Legal Almanac Series No. 68

AUTOMOBILE LIABILITY AND THE CHANGING LAW

by M. G. Woodroof III
Assistant Professor of Law, Drake University
School of Law

and Alphonse M. Squillante
Professor of Law, Associate Dean, Drake University
School of Law

1972 OCEANA PUBLICATIONS, INC.
Dobbs Ferry, New York

This is the sixty-eighth number in a series of LEGAL ALMANACS which bring you the law on various subjects in nontechnical language. These books do not take the place of your attorney's advice, but they can introduce you to your legal rights and responsibilities.

Library of Congress Cataloging in Publication Data

Woodroof, M. G.   1939-
     Automobile liability and the changing law.

     (Legal almanac series, no. 68)
     1.   Insurance, Automobile--U. S. I. Squillante,
Alphonse M.,   1932-   joint author. II. Title.
KF1218.Z9W6   346'.73'086   75-39041
ISBN 0-379-11082-2

ACKNOWLEDGEMENT

Many thanks to Mrs. Patricia Miller, our secretary, and John S. Congalton, our research assistant (second year law student). Their hard work and dedication has made this book possible.

M.G.W., III
A.M.S.

CONTENTS

Chapter One

THE PRESENT SYSTEM OF
AUTOMOBILE ACCIDENT REPARATIONS

Historical Evolution of the System

The present system of automobile accident reparations is neither unitary nor simple, but results from the complex inter-action of several different legal and sociological mechanisms. One of the most basic of these mechanisms, frequently, though inaccurately, described as the basis of the present system, is a form, particularly adaptable to the automobile accident situation, of Anglo-American jurisprudence known as "tort law." Under the principles of negligence as applied under tort law, a citizen inflicting injury upon another citizen, not (or only incidentally) in violation of the criminal law, is answerable to that injured party to the extent of the damages inflicted. The law, by operating in this fashion, is designed to produce an interwoven pattern of favorable effects.

First, the injured party is indemnified. By requiring the party who as the result of his negligence is responsible for the injured party's damages to pay to him the amount of those damages, the injured party is compensated, and is, hopefully, restored to the same position as he held prior to the infliction of the injury. In furtherance of this particular goal, the purpose of the tort law has been described as "making the victim whole again," and other collateral doctrines supportive of this premise such as the requirement that the responsible party must pay for any damages attributable to the individual character of the injured party ("you take the victim as you find him") have been developed. An entirely separate area of the law damages has grown up around the questions involved in computing the actual amount of retribution to be paid in individual cases.

Second, the party responsible for the injuries, the wrong-doer, known as the tort-feasor, is punished for his unlawful action. To the extent that compensation is awarded the victim, the tort-feasor is punished in much the same way as is accomplished by the "fine" under the criminal law. The cost, under the tort law, of course, is predicated upon the damage to the victim, on the assumption that the size of the damages will bear some reasonable relationship to the "wrongfulness" of the act causing those damages.

Third, the threat of being found responsible for the injuries of another, under the tort law, has been presumed to act as a deterrent to the sort of behavior which might result in that type of liability. To the extent that this deterrent effect operates, the social goal of controlling individual behavior to conform within reasonable, social limits, will have been attained, at a cost considerably less than that of achieving the same goal by use of criminal law sanctions.

Fourth, the cost of compensation of victims of this sort of behavior is shifted, assuming that such cost must be assumed as a social burden, from the shoulders of society in general and placed instead upon the shoulders of the tort-feasor, as the individual primarily responsible for the damages. Thus the party responsible for creating the _need_ for the compensation bears the greatest burden of the _cost_ of the compensation, reducing the burden upon society.

Fifthly, the injured party is enabled, through operation of the tort law, to achieve a degree of "retribution" or "vengence" against the wrong-doer. The direct confrontation, in the lawsuit, between the victim and the tort-feasor, serves to provide the victim with emotional, as well as financial satisfaction, and this is presumed to lessen the degree to which the victim is likely to resort to self-help in this regard.

The basics for the application of these tort law principles to the automobile situation are simple. To the extent to which a party to an automobile accident is proven to be unlawfully responsible for damages to another party, the injured party may institute a lawsuit "in tort" to recover against the responsible party the amount of those damages. The nature of the "unlawfulness" of the actions of the responsible party may vary, of course, but nearly always in the automobile accident situation, "unlawfulness" is based upon "negligence" or failure to perform in a manner as would be expected of a reasonably prudent person under the circumstances. The doctrine of the "reasonably prudent man" has developed and evolved hand-in-hand with the larger body of tort law, as the standard of care which must be met in order to avoid a finding of negligence. Many collateral and supportive doctrines (such as <u>res ipsa loquitur</u>, i.e. "the thing speaks for itself"); or <u>negligence per se</u>, i.e. "the act was negligent in and of itself") have been developed in regard to the determination of what duty of care is required of a motorist under the "reasonably prudent man" doctrine.

The primary limitations upon the operation of the tort law, in automobile accident situations as well as other situations, revolve around the protection afforded the alleged tort-feasor. In every case, even though the aforementioned doctrines may be incorporated in order to make the job easier, the wrongfulness of the actions of the accused party must be provable and proven in a court of law. To the extent, then, that some accidents may occur as the result of factors not including the wrongfulness of one of the parties involved, but to actions the existence or wrongfulness of which cannot be proven, the tort law will not work in aid of the victim.

The second of the primary basis of the present system of automobile insurance reparation is "direct insurance" (the differences between "direct insurance" and "third-party insurance," of no importance to this initial description of insurance operation, will be discussed later) which has developed as an economic mechanism to lessen the extreme variations of risk regarding the probabilities of individual disaster as the result of fortuitous occurrences. There are certainly occurrences in life which, without any precisely determinable predictability, cause their unfortunate consequences to be brought to bear upon certain (a limited number of) individuals to the exclusion of others, and which can be expected to recur with a frequency which is actuarially, though not individually, predictable. Insurance, as an economic mechanism for enabling individuals to protect themselves from the disaster accompanying such misfortunes, enables a group of individuals who may potentially be effected by such an occurrence to pool their resources in the buildup of funds sufficient to compensate for damage to those of their number who actually, prospectively, fall victim to the particular hazard concerned. Thus each member of the group is subject to the loss (i.e., having to pay) of a small sum, but is protected from the consequences of the very large loss in the event that he is one of the particular individuals who is ultimately subject to untoward incident. The theory behind this manner of spreading the risk to provide protection for certain involved individuals is called "the insurance principle." In order for a particular hazard to be a subject fit for insurance, it must have the following characteristics:

1. Economic consequences of its occurrence, as applied to a large group of people, must be predictable. This is called "the law of large numbers."

2. It must not be predictable or controllable in terms of whether it will befall or not befall any certain individual. Stated another way, this means that there must be an ascertainable group of individuals concerning each of whom the probabilities of the incident occurring are similar and less than certain, (life insurance meets this criteria, not because the predictability of death as to any individual is questionable - it is, of course, certain - but rather because the predictability of premature death is not so predictable), with only a few individuals - out of the large group - actually likely to suffer the consequences of the occurrence of the incident.

3. The economic consequences of the occurrence must be sufficiently disastrous as to warrant creation of an insurance mechanism in order to provide protection against their effect.

4. The frequency of the occurrence must be sufficiently low that the cost of creating the requisite pool, when spread among all the members of the group, is not prohibitive. (It is for failure to meet this requirement, for instance, that earthquake insurance, and flood insurance, and insurance against the consequences of war have not proven feasible.)

It is easy to see that several facets of the automobile accident problem fit the above characteristics, and are therefore subject to the potential of the insurance mechanism. The consequences of personal injury (including death) may be protected against by participation in plans of life insurance, in any of its many forms, any of the various kinds of health and hospitalization insurance, any of the various forms of accident insurance, or, with particular reference to the automobile accident situation, the death benefits, disability benefits, or medical payments benefits in the standard automobile insurance policy, the Family Auto Policy (or F.A.P.). The consequences of damage to the motor vehicle itself can be protected against by participation in any of various insurance schemes designed to meet this need, particularly through the comprehensive and collision insurance portions of the F.A.P.

It is important to realize that insurance, unlike the working of the tort law system described earlier, does not operate in such a manner as to shift the cost of compensation of victims back upon those responsible for the damage, but rather spreads it amongst those parties in the position of potentially suffering such a loss. In the former case, the tort law system, because the recipient of the burden of paying the compensation is the wrongdoer, he is held individually responsible for the entire burden. In the case of insurance, however, because all the recipients of this burden are presumably blameless, each member of the group sustains only a small _pro rata_ portion of the burden. The present system of automobile accident reparation, then, rests upon dual bases: the tort system _and_ the principle of insurance. Under the tort law system, a party has a legal right to bring suit and recover full compensation for his individual damages against any party legally responsible for having caused those damages. To the extent to which an individual might suffer damages not the fault of any other party (through his own, or partly through his own fault, for example), or as the result of an accident the cause of which is not provable in court, or whose damages are in excess of the financial resources of the wrongdoer, he may provide for these contingencies through the means of insurance.

It is unfortunate but clearly true that the present systems of reparation for automobile accident injuries and losses do not serve primarily to reduce the amount or effect of those losses, but merely to redistribute the burdens created by the accident situation. Direct insurance, as a matter of fact, might conceivably have the effect of increasing the accident hazard, inasmuch as it provides the mechanism whereby the results of an accident, even in those situations where the accident is caused by clearly preventable negligence, are somewhat abrogated. Thus, an individual who is insured has less reason to drive safely than an individual who is uninsured, because the consequences of an accident for the insured victim would be less onerous.

Not much attention has been paid to the notion that insurance serves to lessen the amount of pressure encouraging safe driving, however, because it has been assumed that the threat of the consequences of an accident, even when compensation is available through insurance, is sufficient in itself to spur a degree of safe driving. The tort system, however, has utilized the reverse of this situation in order to increase the deterrence of unsafe driving, to the degree to which that may be possible. Even though a driver may be somewhat deterred from activities involving a risk of accident by that very risk, even though compensation through insurance may be available, and may be deterred to perhaps a greater degree by that risk if accompanied by knowledge of the fact that no compensation will be available, his potential antisocial behavior will be even more deterred in the event that he might have to fear the consequences not only of his own involvement in the accident, but also that of other parties involved. This, of course, is the result of accident litigation and of the tort system. The party responsible for the accident not only must bear his own losses, lessened by the degree to which compensation through insurance is available to him, but must also bear the losses of the other parties injured in the accident, which will be shifted upon him by the tort system.

It is entirely likely that in some such situations, the burden of the losses of other parties involved, shifted through the tort system, becomes by far the most significant burden. It may be that the party responsible for the accident has suffered no significant injuries of his own, but finds that the financial burden of compensating other victims of the accident resulting from his negligence amounts to financial disaster. This risk, then - that is, the risk of becoming financially responsible for the loss of other parties in an accident for which a driver is found negligent - is itself a risk meeting all the criteria for the application of insurance. It is almost certain to occur, with great predictability when dealing with large groups of people; it is of great significance to the individual upon whom it falls; and it is not accurately predictable in any individual case. Therefore, the insurance principle, just as it has been applied to the accident risk itself, has been applied to this risk, which can be termed the "liability risk," and such insurance is called "liability insurance."

Liability insurance is insurance protecting the insured individual from the risk of financial disaster ensuing from his being found liable for injuries to others resulting from an accident of which he has been determined to be the cause. Abuses of the legal technicalities inherent in such a situation led, in the early history of the development of this type of insurance, to the practice of paying, through the insurance medium, the benefits of the insurance directly to the injured party "on behalf" of the insured individual, rather than merely paying the insurance as reimbursement to the negligent party as "first party" after he has paid, out of his own finances, the judgment due the victim. As the result of these developments, the typical liability insurance situation involves an insurer, the insured person, and a third party, the victim of the accident, to whom the insured is liabile, and to whom the benefits of the insurance are ultimately paid. The presence of this third party has led to the labeling of this type of insurance as "third-party insurance," as contrasted with direct, or "first-party" insurance.

Liability insurance has proven to be a boon for the victim of the accident as well as for the insured individual. Often the assets of the insured party exist in some nonliquid form, are difficult to ascertain, are questionable in value or are nonexistent. The proceeds of a liability insurance contract, on the other hand, are readily available and payable in cash. Because of this, and of the very high degree to which liability insurance has saturated the market place, the nature of the liability insurance contract has become blurred, so that it is now thought of more often in terms of protection for the potential victim of the accident than as a contract providing protection for the party found liable. Indeed, under this conceptualization, liability insurance has actually become a bit of a hybrid, serving as direct insurance taken out on behalf of the victim (who surely exists as an individual or individuals, even though his actual identity is not established until after the fact), paid for by the tort-feasor (in advance, of course), and subject to the limitation, in collection, that the beneficiary must prove the liability of the insurance purchaser. Perhaps, had not liability insurance existed to so well serve this need, a special insurance contract of this very nature might have well been developed.

Because of this dual nature of the liability insurance contract, liability insurance has come to be viewed, in its social setting, as protection for a potential victim, even more than as protection against the consequences of liability. Consequently, this system of liability insurance has become, to many, synonymous with the entire system of reparation for automobile insurance injuries. Nothing could be further from the truth. The primary bases of the totality of our present system of automobile accident reparations are, in <u>combination</u>, the systems of tort law and direct insurance. Liability insurance is merely a collateral development, the importance of which grows not out of its importance in the interworkings of the system so much as out of the pervasiveness of its occurrence.

Societal systemic interaction, not the application of tort law, makes the present method of reparation for automobile accident victims complex. Tort law is the foundation of today's reparation model. Though commonly thought to be so, tort law is <u>not</u> the fount of all reparations. It is only <u>one</u> of a series of reparations systems by which recovery for an injury or loss may be had.

Tort law shifts the burden of loss arising out of an injury from the victim to the party responsible for causing the injury. It seems only fair (and historically has seemed only fair) to place the party causing the injury or damage in the position of making the innocent party whole. However, the system of providing reparation for the injured party by suing in tort is not the only way to compensate the automobile accident victim. To the extent that society provides any other legal tool by which an injured party can recover for his damages, the needs of society are also met.

There are some needs which society meets, but it does not and cannot meet all the needs of all its automobile driving citizens. The major problem in a burden-shifting tort system is that the shift is often made from one party who cannot take the loss to another party who may be in as poor a position. To shift the loss to a tort-feasor unable to satisfy the demands of the injured party is a useless, frustrating, legal fiction.

In the event of loss, society's choices are to permit the injured party to bear the loss, with no recovery permitted against the wrongdoer (obviously an unfair, unsound public policy), or to shift the loss to the wrongdoer and expect him to pay for his wrongdoing (obviously a risky public policy), or to provide some method of compensation from general revenues of society (interesting but impractical), or to encourage a system whereby a stranger to the parties agrees to satisfy the needs of the victim and at the same time prevent economic tragedy for the driver and owner who may have caused the injury (the role of an insurer).

8

Automobile liability insurance, financial responsibility laws, and cash bonds are alternative means by which our society allows the tort-feasor and innocent party alike to protect themselves. It is not often that the tort-feasor bears the burden of the shift of risk of loss because the liability insurer is the bearer. Nor must the system break down if the tort-feasor is uninsured and financially irresponsible, because the innocent party usually has the benefit of uninsured motorist protection. Hospitalization and various other medical benefits may be paid directly to the victim, on a first-party insurance basis, regardless of fault.

Group health, hospitalization and life plans are so pervasive in our society that it is unlikely that the victims are without the means to be compensated for injuries received in an automobile accident. Even if these plans are not provided for the consumer, and he does not opt to buy automobile insurance coverage, if he is a wage earner or elderly person he is most likely covered by Social Security, Medicare, Workmen's Compensation, or an endless variety of governmental or employer-provided protection plans, all of which compensate him for his loss and all of which work with the tort system, not against it. Such reparations systems probably compensate 80-90% of all accident victims.

Still further, the victim may have chosen not to be covered by an insurance policy or to rely on litigation to make him whole; such individuals may rely on their personal savings, their family, their church, or other charitable organizations to meet their needs, and so do not seek redress in the tort or insurance system.

Further, given the improvidence of man, there is still another provision to meet the needs of society. In the event that the victim may not have purchased first-party insurance, he may still be able to collect in tort, even if the defendant is uninsured and judgment-proof, through an "unsatisfied judgment fund."

Our system is a tort system plus alternatives - all stressing the prevention of financial catastrophies. The interlocking solutions available to the injured party make the destruction of our present system unnecessary. Evolution from the present tort system is possible and preferable.

Even in the event that the automobile accident victim cannot enforce a tort claim or indeed was at fault himself, he can still obtain some reparation through his first-party insurance coverage. To go unrecompensed the accident victim must suffer from an incredible combination of breakdowns in society's reparation systems. To remain unpaid he must be unable to prove fault in a tort suit, or have not purchased uninsured motorist protection, or have declined to purchase medical payments coverage available on the Family Automobile Policy, or have no accident and health insurance available to him, or have no group insurance plans, or not be covered by some government insurance program covering his type of accident, or have failed to provide for such emergencies with personal savings, or be unable to rely on his family for help, or be unable to obtain help from various charitable organizations.

Evolutionary improvement of the present system provides a rational approach for meeting and solving the needs which are not presently met. For a victim to have no source of recovery under our present system requires a deliberate avoidance of his part of available remedies through which recovery is possible.

The Goals of the Present System

The present system is the result of many centuries of development of Anglo-American law. The system has incorporated and maintained certain definite goals of the society in which it has developed and thrived. These incorporated societal goals are too often overlooked in critical evaluations of the system.

The primary goal of the existing reparation system is the preservation of the right of each individual to use his own judgment to determine the priorities applicable to the allocation of his resources. Attacks upon this right are not of recent origin. Indeed, Anglo-American legal history has oftentimes imposed a "Strict liability" principle so that any actor would be liable for any losses resulting from his actions. However, it is notable that even in the early cases where strict liability was imposed, the loss would not be shifted to or upon the actor himself, but rather through him - as an instrumentality - to other societal units who were either better situated to bear or distribute the loss or more "responsible" for the loss. After a time the law changed so that proof of "no negligence" would relieve the actor of liability despite the earlier reasoning and, still later, evolved to allow the victim to recover only upon positive proof of neg-

ligence. Then in more recent years, the early reasoning was re-
asserted. Workmen's Compensation laws are relatively modern
examples of the reversion to strict liability. Under such laws
an employer may be held strictly liable, without proof of negligence, for injuries to his employees, on the principle that he will
incorporate the cost of paying such compensation into his cost of
doing business, and therefore pass his losses on to the consumers of his produce. The inapplicability of this principle (of pass-
ing on" the costs, as a mere instrumentality) to the individuals
making up the motoring public is clear justification, both histor-
ical and present, for the particular negligence-oriented shifting
of the burden of accident loss which evolved as an improvement
upon this early law and developed into our present tort law system.

A second goal of the system, then, operating through the tort
law, is the morally acceptable allocation of cost. The entire
negligence law concept is designed to determine when the cost of
accidents should be allowed to fall upon the victim of the accident
and when those costs should be so shifted as to fall upon the negligent party. In the event that there is no provable negligence
on the part of some party other than the victim, or that it cannot
be proven that such negligence is the proximate cause of the damage, the loss will not be shifted. The tort law system is an initial deviation from the earlier principle, so that this one narrow
class of losses, those resulting from the provable negligence of
another party, is shifted from the victim to the negligent party.

A third goal of the system was made possible as a collateral
result of the development of the tort law as a determinant of when
the loss should or should not be shifted. As a result of the operation of tort law principles, each case is treated on its own individual merits. An additional, previously unmentioned, principle of the law in this area is "the tort-feasor takes the victim
as he finds him." This principle is invoked in these cases to
avoid any stereo typed measures of negligence, liability or damages, and the individual case-by-case analysis which has become typical of the operation of the tort law system in this regard is universally recognized as one of our greatest accomplish-
ments in the creation of humanitarian principles of law.

The fourth goal of the present system is an extension of the
individual case-by-case treatment described above. In each
tort case, if recovery is allowed at all, the avowed purpose of

the law is to provide full, individually tailored recovery to the victim. Where possible, the victim is to be "made whole again." The damages are to be assessed in his individual case according to his individual circumstances, and awarded accordingly.

A fifth goal of the existing automobile accident reparation system is the provision of options to individuals so that those individuals whose losses do not result from the provable negligence of another party will be enabled to provide for their potential needs through methods other than the tort law system. Therefore, protection has been made available to those individuals who choose to purchase it in the form of liability insurance (against the possibility of being economically ruined by a tort judgment) and first-party accident and health insurance (as protection against the direct consequences of loss to oneself as the result of injuries received in an accident). Automobile insurance "medical payments" benefits, health and hospitalization insurance, disability insurance, income continuation insurance, and life insurance are common examples of such coverages.

It is up to the individual himself to determine how he will allocate his resources to provide against the economic tragedy of being either a victim of a tort-feasor, inasmuch as he must realize that the probabilities of his falling into either category are largely functions of his own behavior. An individual may choose to pay premiums in any combination for various first-party or liability insurance coverages available to him (thereby purchasing "peace of mind" and protection against loss, to the extent that insurance can provide), or the individual may choose to allocate his money for other purposes, thereby self-insuring himself in regard to these kinds of losses. The entire system is designed to allow the individual this autonomy in determining his priorities, in opposition to the possibility of making these determinations for him against his will and in derogation of his individually determined priorities.

It has been previously noted that the tort-imposed shift of loss to the negligent actor is designed to induce behavior in individuals which is acceptable and compatible with social demands upon his behavior. The tort system is a complement to the criminal law in that the threat of liability and accompanying lawsuit is designed as a deterrent against negligent behavior. In this regard, however, it has been suggested that very few individuals are likely deterred from negligent behavior by the threat of a tort suit resulting from an automobile accident. Other considerations of much greater vitality are said to arise from careless driving, so that the additional deterrent effect of the operation of the tort law system is secondary. For example, it has been suggested that it is unlikely that an individual would be primarily deterred from negligent behavior by the threat of a lawsuit, and the possibility of accompanying economic ruin, since his main concern must be the risk of severe bodily injury and economic harm to himself resulting therefrom. In the final analysis, it would appear that <u>neither</u> of these eventualities would reliably and effectively operate as a severe deterrent to negligent driving. Human experience leads to the clear understanding that uncertain and remote punishment, regardless of potential severity, has very little effect in deterring anti-social behavior.

Clearly the possibility of being killed or severely injured in an automobile accident is of <u>some</u> deterrent effect, as is the possibility of financial hardship resulting from a tort suit, but the effect from either must be slight. Even though the very thought of such an occurrence is abhorrent to the average person, the <u>probabilities</u> against such an occurrence happening to any one individual are even more impressive to him. Statistics pointing out the accident-per-mile-driven rate only generate a feeling of complacency, despite the horror inherent in the severity of the potential injuries.

It is doubtful that most drivers are deterred from reckless driving because of any fear that such behavior may result in a tort law negligence suit and the resulting financial liability. That fear is overcome because the probability is very great that such a tort judgment will not be rendered, and also the individual may protect himself from the ruinous potentialities of even such an unlikely occurrence by obtaining liability insurance. Or the driver may simply recognize and rely upon the principle that he is judgment-proof. In any event he will not be severely hurt by any tort judgment rendered against him. This fact merely compounds the unlikelihood of being found negligent in such a way as to lessen even more the deterrent impact. Such a deterrent must exist, in theory, but it is likely to be of no real effectiveness. A deterrent which hits much closer to home is being classified for insurance purposes as a high-risk driver (defined as "a driver presenting a high risk of causing through tort law his liability insurance carrier to have to pay a claim"), who very likely must pay either higher insurance premiums, or be unable to obtain insurance with the company of his choice. Here there is invoked a punishment, not exceedingly great, but relatively certain and severe enough that when combined with probability, acts as a deterrent to unacceptable behavior. Therefore, the tort law system in combination with the insurance system, can be seen to operate, through this phenomenon, rather effectively to induce non-negligent human behavior, and as such is also a complement to the criminal law system. Tort law serves this function at a cost which is borne by the insured public, to be sure, but which is much less than the cost involved in enforcement of the criminal law per se. This particular goal of the present system, and its effectiveness, must therefore be considered in any analysis of the cost of the present system, as well as of the operation of the present system.

Another goal of the present system, understandable only by consideration of the operation and interaction of the system as a whole, is the rational allocation of costs. The tort system, with the accompanying insurance risk classification plans, assures allocation of costs among members of society in a way which is proportionate to the degree to which those members contribute to the problem. In liability insurance, for example, negligent drivers, to the extent to which they can be identified, located and classified, are usually charged much higher rates than "safe" drivers. The higher insurance rate is charged because liability insurers will probably have to pay victims more often and a greater amount as a result of claims based on the activities of these drivers, than upon the basis of fewer and smaller claims resulting from the activities of the safe drivers. Classification plans operate to allocate these costs proportionately not only upon the basis of proven negligence, but also upon the basis of geographical area, use of the vehicle, characteristics of the drivers, and such other criteria as may be developed with actuarial soundness consistent with the law of large numbers. To the extent that these factors may be statistically shown to add to the risks of travel on our highways, a higher proportion of the costs of motoring is shifted thereunto. This extra cost will then be reflected in the decisions of the motoring public as reflected in their support of better highway design, better vehicle design, and other methods of reducing the slaughter on the highways, both as it applies to _their_ insurance rates and in general. This additional shifting of costs serves, directly or indirectly, depending upon the specific factor involved, to deter the continuation of these risk-producing circumstances.

The same principles operate in the allocation of motoring costs through the rating mechanisms of first-party insurers. Those individuals who because of personal characteristics or predelictions to loss are more likely to make demands upon the insurance pool under their first-party insurance coverages are generally rated "higher" than those individuals who are least likely to make such demands. This is nothing more than the extension of the previously described rating practices applied in the first-party insurance context, and once again represents a rational allocation of the cost. The present system, to the extent that the tort system shifts costs from victims to negligent drivers (at least as a class), and to the extent that it allocates cost proportionately among the continuum from the least likely claimant under the first-party insurance policy to the most likely claimant, furthers the express goal of rationally allocating costs.

How the System Operates
____

There are certain characteristics of the present system which provide additional benefits over and above those which are integrally incorporated into the system itself. Some emphasis has been placed upon the shortcomings involved in the functioning of the present system; such emphasis is not helpful unless the full picture, including the _strength_ derived from the functioning of the system, is considered.

First, it is a simple fact that under the present system, most people (80-90%) _do_ in fact receive _some_ compensation for their injuries, regardless of the presence or absence of provable negligence in the accident. Many persons receive compensation under the tort system even though they may not have valid or provable tort claims. To the extent that this may represent overpaid nuisance claims, it is unfortunate, but to the extent that it represents compromise recoveries in cases of doubtful negligence, it represents, overall, an extension of the degree to which the operation of the tort law provides for the compensation of automobile accident victims.

Other individuals recover as a result of first-party insurance, which may take the form of "medical payments" insurance or private health, accident or disability insurance. Still other individuals recover under group insurance policies or under the various forms of governmental insurance. Others recover as a result of the efforts of charitable, fraternal, or familial organizations.

It is possible for an individual to recover under first-party insurance coverages as well as, and in addition to, the principles of tort law, in accordance with the "Collateral Source Doctrine." The "Collateral Source Doctrine" provides that evidence of compensation from collateral sources is not to be considered in determination of the amount of damages recoverable in a tort action against an allegedly negligent motorist. Despite the fact that there has been much controversy about this doctrine, empirical evidence suggests that most victims, particularly those with serious injuries and losses, recover ultimately somewhat less than all their losses; thus the "Collateral Source Doctrine," rather than most often providing for double recovery, merely enables these victims to be more nearly fully compensated for the loss which they have sustained. Furthermore, it can be forcefully argued that first-party insurance is an economic commodity, a "product" which is purchased and paid for, from which there should be a recovery in the event of loss regardless of other considerations, such as recovery against a negligent motorist responsible for their injuries.

A crucial problem in automobile accident compensation is not so much that certain victims go uncompensated, but rather the fact that nearly all victims who suffer catastrophic losses are compensated to a degree representative of only a small percent of those losses. Obviously the problems of these victims need greater attention.

As it actually functions, the present system is so designed that virtually all valid tort judgments are usually ultimately enforceable. If the nominal defendant is judgment-proof, he has very likely purchased liability insurance. The scope of such coverage in force ranges from approximately 70-98% of all eligible motorists in our fifty states, with the percentage in most states falling nearer the latter mark. As a result, it is very likely that any judgment rendered against a negligent motorist will be paid by a liability insurance carrier, even in the event that the individual defendant is judgment-proof.

If such a defendant is judgment-proof and uninsured as well, the victim may recover against his own insurer if he has purchased uninsured motorist protection, which is available in all states and mandatory in some. In the extreme unlikely event that the defendant is both judgment-proof and uninsured and the victim himself has not obtained uninsured motorist protection, a tort judgment must be collectible in some other manner if the total reliability of the system is to be assured. This last-ditch collectability has not proven difficult to provide. The unsatisfied judgment funds which have been created in some states are an example of one method of meeting this need.

The chances of collectibility on a tort judgment are correlative to possible accident involvement. This fact is based on available empirical evidence which tends to indicate that the very drivers who are judgment-proof are also those who are likely to be uninsured, and that these very same drivers are those most likely to be involved in accidents. The evidence in support of the above statement is not clear, but even if true this unfortunate trend is ameliorated through the application of the financial responsibility laws which are prevalent throughout the United States. Financial responsibility laws, in general, require that an individual who has shown himself, in accordance with the variable standards imposed by the states, to present a high risk of incurring and failing to satisfy a tort liability, must demonstrate proof of financial responsibility in order to retain his license to drive. Usually, required financial responsibility is provided in the form of automobile liability insurance. These laws have assured that the individuals most likely to incur tort liability are not quite so likely to be uninsured as they might otherwise be according to the possibilities just mentioned.

Another example of the functioning of the present system to overcome apparent deficiencies is presented by the several methods employed in order to ascertain that all motorists do in fact become active participants in the present system. The operation of financial responsibility laws has already been mentioned, and assigned risk plans have not only been examined previously but will be reviewed later. In addition, three states (New York, Massachusetts, and North Carolina)have enacted legislation providing that liability insurance be required of all motorists as a matter of law. Such legislation is of course an extreme effort to assure that all drivers will be included in the present system. As might be expected, perfection has not been achieved in that regard, and other states have achieved a higher percentage of insured motorists with solutions other than compulsory insurance. These other states are illustrations of the effectiveness of the functioning of the present system as an inducement to participation in the system by all motorists.

Financial responsibility laws allow an uninsured motorist "the first bite." By the same token, they allow those motorists who have not demonstrated any appreciably high risk of negligent driving on the highways, or of financial irresponsibility, the freedom of choice to allocate their resources in accordance with their own wishes. To the extent that such drivers ultimately become liable in tort for a first time and unable to satisfy that liability, they represent not a unique automobile insurance problem, but rather a social problem. Even so, the existing automobile accident reparation system includes provisions assuring that such claims may be satisfied by the methods described already. The costs of filling this need have been allocated among motorists proportionately on the basis of contribution to the risk, along with the other costs of the system.

The tort law and insurance systems operate largely through the American judicial process. Objective analysis indicates that the adversary and judicial systems have not worked particularly unsatisfactorily in this context. There has been much discussion concerning the degree to which excessive delay is inherent in the process of bringing tort litigation cases to trial. It cannot be questioned that such delay exists in certain jurisdictions, or that within those jurisdictions the delay proves harmful to prompt operation of the insurance system as it has been described. Where the problem exists, therefore, it <u>affects</u> the automobile insurance system, but it definitely is <u>not created</u> by the automobile insurance system. Research indicates that the over-crowding characteristic of the dockets of the courts in the jurisdictions affected is the result not of civil actions, but of a great increase in the <u>criminal</u> caseload of these courts; thus no change in the automobile insurance system can have great effect upon this delay.

The answer to court delay is not to redesign the automobile insurance system to adapt to the malfunctioning judicial process
but, rather, to correct the judicial process so that it will be enabled to successfully and adequately meet the need of providing
justice to the litigants making up its criminal caseload as well
as its automobile insurance caseload.

To this end, judicial reform has proven, wherever seriously promulgated, to be a successful remedy to the problem of delay in court litigation. Note well that all available evidence indicates that the court delay problem is serious only in a few specific large metropolitan areas in the United States, but is a minimal problem throughout the remainder of the length and breadth
of the land. It is a fact that most jurisdictions do not suffer from
this problem, and that proposals to correct this problem by possible changes in the automobile insurance system are both unnecessary and implausible.

"Costs" represent another element which must be considered
in conjunction with the operation of the judicial and adversary systems as a part of the machinery in furtherance of the automobile
insurance plan as an entirety. Court costs, as such, have not
been often mentioned as an excessive burden in this regard, even
though the fees involved in appealing from the arbitration courts
in Pennsylvania (some $75-$100) has been unsuccessfully attacked
as possibly unconstitutional. The more serious problem in the
area, of course, or at least the problem more often discussed,
involves the contingent fee system utilized by the trial Bar. The
attacks upon the 'contingent fee system frequently center around
the apparent unfairness of the system in providing for fees of up
to one-third of the final judgment or settlement in the very large
cases. There is usually never any attempt to analyze the actual
amount of work (such as would be billed on the more usual hour-
ly basis) which has been expended in the handling of these cases;
nor is there an examination of the expenses incurred by the attorney. It would appear oftentimes to be merely assumed that
such a fee must be unreasonable. Inasmuch as other types of
cases are not often so extended in time, expensive in the use of
expert testimony, or otherwise as demanding of specific expertise as the average automobile case, it is clear that a tort judgment must be very large before a one-third contingency fee is
necessarily unreasonable. At the same time, the contingency

fee in the smaller cases can hardly be considered to be out of line
at one-third, for such fees are perhaps the only method by which
the clients having these smaller cases would be able to obtain
satisfactory legal representation.

The System Evaluated

For every gain, in terms of human values, attained by the
creation of any mechanism designed to deal with social problems,
there must be a loss of the opposite value. Greater liberty, for
example, means less security, in the narrow sense, and vice ver-
sa. The same reasoning can be applied to our system of automobile accident reparations, and indeed, many of the attacks
upon this system in recent times have been so rooted. The system retains the implementation of the values upon which it was
built, and has not noticeably changed, while the values upon which
it is based have come to be reexamined.

The assumption has been that those whose conduct leads to
automobile accidents should bear the greater part of the financial
burden created by those accidents; that there are "innocent" and
"guilty" parties in reference to automobile accidents. In general
terms, the conflict which has led to the attacks upon the present
system is that which exists between this particular value concept
of "justice" upon which the present system is based - obtaining
compensation for the innocent by charging responsibility to the
guilty while providing voluntary opportunity through insurance
for greater security than is thus afforded - and the very different
value concept of justice which is held by many modern critics
of the system - compulsory participation, without option except
as to the extent of certain "additional" coverages, in a social
scheme designed to provide partial compensation for all, innocent or guilty, with ultimate responsibility and costs to be levied
upon "society at large," or, in other words, every individual
citizen as a member of that society, regardless of innocence or
guilt.

These new value positions incorporate, inherently, the fac-
tual assumptions that there is no real distinction, or means of
determining the difference, between the "innocent" and the "guilt-
y;" that the costs attendant on making such determinations are
expensive and wasteful; and that our social duty to the "guilty,"

based upon the above assumptions cannot be differentiated from our social duty to the "innocent."

Because of the highly controversial nature of these changes in value position, which are clearly accepted by some members of our society and not by others, the attack upon the present system has been further based upon alleged inefficiencies in the system's ability to accomplish the purposes for which it is intended. Thus it is claimed that the social mechanisms utilized by our present system of reparations are not sufficiently competent and efficient, in and of themselves, that they may be profitably utilized in furthering the social goals for which the system is intended. Thus, it is said even if the goals and strengths of the present system would be of social utility if possible of accomplishment, the present operation of our insurance companies, claims investigation organization, court systems, lawyers and legal system, and the social awareness of each individual citizen, function at such a low level that, in conjunction, they defeat the entire purpose of the system.

In order for the present system to implement its goals it is necessary that it function in a reasonably efficient manner. To the extent to which it functions inefficiently we have its greatest weakness. Does the system function reasonably and efficiently when it is tested by an accident resulting from the negligent operation of a motor vehicle?

It has been speculated that negligent operation of motor vehicles is not a fundamental reason for the occurrence of automobile accidents in our society. It has been reasoned that such accidents occur because of the large number of automobiles upon the highways, because of normal human weaknesses on the part of drivers, because of the various manipulative skills necessary for handling today's automobile, because of poor highway or automobile design, or because of any combination of these factors. This proposition, not borne out by empirical evidence, will be examined in some detail later.

Assuming for the moment that there is a degree of negligence involved in most automobile accidents, is this negligence provable in court? It has not been established that determination of negligence, or lack of it, is so speculative in nature, so self-serving in import, so fraught with the possibility of perjury, so unlikely to be an accurate report of what happened at the time of the accident, so subject to the possibility of bribery, so unreliable in description by any witness, or so complicated by the impact of the accident are the victim as to be impossible. Yet all of these charges have been made. Even <u>with</u> these factors it may not be said with any certainty that no jury in a court of law can make a reasonable interpretation of what is negligent motor vehicle operation. There is no evidence that the automobile accident insurance claim problem is so unique from all other problems tried in courts of law that it alone should be subject to the charge that is causing a malfunction in our system.

For the present system, as for <u>any</u> system, to function properly, it is essential that the parties to the accident, their attorneys, the court, and the insurance company act in good faith towards one another in seeking a solution to their problem. It has been suggested that the present system encourages fraud and dishonesty on the part of all these parties and that all these parties may fail to meet the test of good faith in attempts to better their own position insofar as the disposition of the claim is concerned. To the extent to which these accusations are true, is it any wonder that the tort law system, or any system suffers? Is there any societal function which can be properly performed in an atmosphere of bad faith? Concomitant with the effacacious functioning of any automobile insurance system must be a restoration of good faith and honesty in all transactions between the parties.

Low limits of coverage, for liability insurance as well as first-party medical coverage, is a problem. In some states liability insurance may provide for as little as $5,000 to any one individual or $10,000 maximum payment for bodily injuries resulting from any single automobile accident. In the majority of states the appropriate limits are only $10,000 and $20,000.

Recovery under the tort system is allowed only where the negligence of the other party is the proximate cause of the accident. The rationale for this feature of the tort system is simply that the risk of loss ought to fall upon the person who caused it if he can be shown to be responsible for the loss as a result of his negligence. Merely because the loss cannot be laid directly to one party it is not intended that the victim should bear the loss alone. The insurance principle operates in such a manner that the victim may spread his risk of loss among a large group of similarly situated individuals. If an individual declines to put himself in such a group, and thereby avoids participation in that spread of risk of loss, he is acting voluntarily, and he cannot lay the blame for his loss upon a malfunction in the automobile insurance system. The present system provides an individual with several alternatives by which he may make a determination as to the degree to which he wishes to allocate his resources in order to protect himself against a loss due to an automobile accident.

Some problems are not designed into the present automobile insurance system, but result from a <u>malfunction</u> of the system. Contingent attorney fees, it has been suggested, represent an abuse of the adversary system. If the contingent fee system, which provides a livelihood for a segment of the American Bar and legal representation for a segment of the American public, serves little or no use except to stir up litigation and bring lawyers into cases where they would otherwise not be needed, then is this a problem which will be cured by changing the system? Contingent fees may be collectible in suits against a first-party insurer just as in suits against a liability insurer.

A goal of the tort system is to provide full compensation to the victim. This lofty moral principle has also been attacked because of the possibility that those individuals with very small claims may be overpaid because of inflated "pain-and-suffering" claims. Rather than go to court the insurance company will pay. This "nuisance claim" concept results from an improper functioning of the system, and the situation needs to be remedied.

It has been suggested that the insurance companies decline to make "advance payments" because they hope, by delay, to force a compromise settlement by the claimant, or because such advance payments would be admissible as evidence of liability in court. These payments would serve to mitigate injuries, to rehabilitate the victim, and to lower the long-range liability of the defendant. If the system functions to prevent these payments, clearly the system needs to be changed.

Another product of the malfunctioning of the present system is that certain people are outside of the operative functioning of the system as we have described it. Some individuals present so high a risk of loss, or a risk of loss that is so indeterminable, that the insurance companies are unable to write insurance coverage, caused mainly by state-imposed rate limitations, to protect them. This problem has been attacked by "assigned risk plans." Under such plans, individuals unable to obtain voluntary coverage written by insurance companies are allowed to obtain coverage under a special plan whereby they are assigned to an individual company to have their insurance written for them. The assignment to such an individual company usually brings higher than normal rates, but not high enough to make these individuals, as a group, self-sustaining. Insofar as the premiums do not accurately reflect the proper classification basis for these individuals, the remainder of the motoring public helps share their risk of loss.

The "insurance principle" requires the pooling of similar risk groups, depending, for implementation, upon a proper rate of classification plan. A second failing of the system is the lack of full implementation of such a classification plan. Rational allocation of costs dictates that those individuals who contribute most directly to the liability risk be rated higher for liability insurance, and those individuals most likely to suffer losses compensable under first-party insurance be more highly rated than others so insured. Under an ultimate classification plan some individuals would be priced completely out of the insurance market - obviously a result which would be contrary to public policy so long as these individuals are allowed to drive. A solution to the problem of those people remaining outside of the system would be to make insurance coverage available to all members of the public, rated in such a manner that each individual would contribute a premium proportionate to his risk.

Unenforceable tort judgments defeat societal needs and the tort principle of placing the victim in the position of being as nearly whole as is possible - to do this the insurance industry and governmental units have created "uninsured motorist protection" and in a few states "unsatisfied judgment funds." A companion of "totally unsatisfied judgments" are those judgments which are in excess of minimum liability insurance policy limits. Such judgments are likely to be uncollectible. Even if the defendant is not judgment-proof, full reparation will seldom be forthcoming in these instances.

It has also been contended that the present system is unworkable in practice because of its dependence upon litigation. It is asserted that the court dockets are so crowded that in many instances the resolution of an automobile accident case is so delayed as to effectively prohibit the victim from relying upon the system; rather, he must settle for "whatever he can get" without waiting for a proper adjudication of the issue. Such court congestion is undoubtedly a problem in some few areas (<u>very</u> few areas) of the country, but is not of widespread significance. In those areas where this is a problem, remedial measures have proven to provide a successful method of resolving the difficulty. Thus, attacks on the present system of reparations, based upon the argument of court congestion, are based upon truth, but subject to greatly misplaced emphasis.

A last attack upon the present system is based upon the possibility of insurance company insolvency. It is argued that just as an individual tort-feasor may be judgment-proof, so an insurance company, through insolvency, might be unable to meet the demands for which it has provided "guarantee." Given the complexity of modern society, it would doubtless be helpful to provide official regulatory assurance protecting against the possibility of loss to automobile victims as a result of insurance company insolvency. Insolvencies, on the other hand, inevitably occur amongst only the very smallest insurance companies, and thereby affect a very small number of policy holders. Traditional insurance industry practice has resulted, through unofficial cooperation amongst participating companies, the protection being afforded such policy holders, even in those rare incidents when insolvency occurred. Thus, the insolvency potential, though properly based in theory, and perhaps profitably subject to official regulation, presents no real basis for substantial attack upon the present system of automobile accident reparation.

The tort system is too frequently singled out as the only method by which a victim could obtain reparation for his injuries. Such singularity results from public ignorance of the operation of our system. Most of the motoring public is unaware of the differences between first-party insurance coverage (such as "medical payments") and liability insurance (which is nearly universal). The American public is not fully aware of its social responsibilities to potential victims; and is somewhat unaware of social and economic necessity for citizens to provide for their own protection. The public is certainly unaware of the totality of legal ramifications of the system. The American public does not approve or disapprove of the system; the public just does not understand the present system.

Moral dynamism is evident in today's society. A portion of the public is moving rapidly towards the principle of collectivism and feels that the "spreading of the loss" is everything. In opposition are those in our society who recognize principles of self-reliance and individual rights, to whom the "spreading of the loss" is not everything. In the middle is the majority of the public, not understanding the entire nature of the arguments of either extreme.

Chapter Two

AUTOMOBILE INSURANCE REFORM

Even though all the countries of the western world share to some degree a common cultural heritage, it is somewhat surprising, given the diversity of life style and government apparatus among those nations, that all of those countries generally share an automobile accident reparations system not greatly dissimilar from the United States' system described heretofore. Yet that is the case.

Of course, certain collateral aspects of the legal systems in these other countries, having an effect upon their automobile insurance reparation system even though not necessarily a direct part of that system, have developed with the purpose of serving the peculiar social values deemed important in those countries, just as certain details of American law have been developed in order to serve the social values in our country. The traditions of social conformity, individual dependence and reliance upon the central state, and a greatly higher tolerance of governmental interference in the ordinary day-to-day affairs of men than would be characteristic of the traditional American ideal, have all served to somewhat simplify the automobile accident reparation problem in these other countries. Without the necessity of placing great value upon individual freedom of action in the allocation of personal resources, complex compulsory governmental schemes have readily been implemented in an attack upon tangible social ills, with much less thought given than would traditionally be required in America to the sacrifice of the intangibles of individual liberty involved in the process.

These other western countries have generally implemented a program of forced governmental social, health, hospitalization and accident insurance. Generally speaking, liability insurance is also compulsory in these countries, regardless of driving record, past history, or other relevant data, and thus there is almost no chance that a suing victim would be financially unable to recover damages. Government sponsored pools have been formed to fill such slight gaps as do in fact exist.

27

Still obviously grounded in the degree to which individual rights are subordinated to the governmental interpretation of the general welfare in some other Western nations to a much greater extent than in the United States, another significant difference between our country and these other Western countries is that their legal systems are much less effectively designed to promote the awarding of appropriate damages to accident victims than is the system in our country. Most often, neither trial by jury nor retention of an attorney on the basis of the contingent fee is allowed.

Given these differences, it is not only somewhat surprising that the automobile accident reparation systems in these Western countries are based upon the same principles of tort liability as heretofore described as providing the basis of the American system, but it is also a good deal easier to understand how those systems might function a good deal "smoother" than the same type of system in the United States. There is considerable danger, however, in equating "smoothness of operation" with "efficiency." In diversity there is strength, as has been demonstrated through the operation of the American constitutional system of individual rights, but in diversity there is also conflict and complication. It is the freedom of the individual to allocate his private resources in such a way as to create a demand for financial responsibility upon the part of potential tort-feasors which creates the need for an effectively operating automobile insurance reparations system which can function to allocate the costs of automobile accidents in a morally and rationally appropriate fashion. It is obvious that elimination of the individual citizen's option is to force elimination of the need, but in social terms such a solution can hardly be deemed efficient. Treating responsible drivers and irresponsible drivers alike, to the extent that all drivers are forced by the government to purchase insurance, obviously serves to effectively eliminate problems generated by irresponsible drivers who fail to meet their social obligation, but the elimination of that problem occurs only as a function of the deprivation of the individual freedom of irresponsible and responsible motorists alike. Lastly, while the operation of legal systems designed to discourage the presentation of claims will greatly alleviate the burden upon the reparations system, it does so only at the expense of the individualized personally tailored damage award that

Americans, with their more personalized standard of justice, have come to expect.

Generally speaking, compensation systems for automobile accidents were established in other western countries some time before this problem came to the active attention of American scholars, and such systems thus serve as the forerunners of the automobile insurance reform movement in the United States. The first really important manifestation of the automobile insurance reform movement in the United States was the Columbia Report of 1932. The Columbia Report regrettably failed to acknowledge the just-mentioned distinction upon which the American system of automobile accident reparations is based, and consequently failed to differentiate between the value choices inherent in the existing system, a politican question, and practical problems created by the malfunctioning under certain circumstances of the existing system, a legitimate object of "reform." Perhaps these oversights can be forgiven in view of the desperate temper of the times during which the Columbia Report was issued. At any rate, although the Columbia Report was never seriously considered for legislative adoption except in four states, it was undoubtedly the object of widespread and intense interest, discussion, and controversy. It was at that time, and remained till 1965, the most important American manifestation of the automobile insurance reform movement.

The most primary and fundamental change advocated in the Columbia Report was the replacement of the various financial responsibility laws in the United States (designed to distinguish as best as possible between an irresponsible and responsible motorist, with the requirement that the irresponsible motorist, though allowed to continue to drive, be allowed to do so only upon presentation of evidence of financial responsibility to meet, at least to some degree, potential claims from torts suits resulting from their negligent driving) with a system of universally compulsory automobile insurance. That is, all motorists, demonstrably responsible and irresponsible alike, would be required by the government to purchase automobile insurance or be denied the right to drive. This feature of the plan was, as we have seen, an American adoption of the principle already previously well established in some other Western countries, abrogating individual freedom and responsibility in favor of collective social legislation. The second significant characteristic of the Columbia Report was that the insurance the obtaining of which was to be compelled was not liability insurance, as has been hereinbefore described, based upon proof of negligence, but rather a form of direct insurance, purchased by the registrant of a motor vehicle for the benefit of any individual suffering personal injuries or death, without regard to fault, caused by the operation of the motor vehicle, achieved by the combination of <u>so-called</u> "liability insurance" with "strict liability, " or liability created in law merely by the existence of the personal injuries or death, rather than by any manifestation of negligence or fault.

The actual payment scheme under the Columbia Report was patterned rather closely after workmen's compensation legislation. Individually tailored compensation for the victim was abolished in favor of a schedule of benefits for particular types of injuries, after the workmen's compensation model, and all compensation for pain and suffering was eliminated.

Despite the interest and controversy aroused by the Columbia Report, it resulted in almost no immediate change in the traditional system of automobile insurance reparations anywhere in the United States, because of several glaring weaknesses. First, the system of scheduled benefits, unacceptable in principle even in the form of workmen's compensation insurance, but tolerable as a matter of political and economic reality in the process of compromising individual victims' rights to recovery with the overall governmental policies of promoting our country's economic development, was even more unacceptable in the case of automobile victims, a group characterized by diversity to a much greater extent than industrial workers and with none of the same over-powering national economic implications. Second, the costs of implementing the Columbia Report proposal were undetermined and the subject of a great deal of controversy.

Thirdly, the Columbia Report itself suffered from doubts concerning the constitutionality of the combination of the two bases of the proposal. The use of the combination of "strict liability" with "liability insurance" in place of the more simple and obvious "direct insurance" was based, at least in part, upon fears that to force a man to insure himself against his own injuries would be constitutionally objectionable. While the idea of requiring compulsory direct insurance has been falsely analogized not only to compulsory liability insurance and to workmens' compensation laws, but also to social security legislation, these analogies do not withstand critical analysis. Constitutional issues involved will be discussed at some length in future chapters.

As the furor created by the Columbia Report diminished somewhat in the United States, in 1946 a plan of compulsory compensation insurance, much like the Columbia Plan, was enacted in the Canadian province of Saskatchewan. The Saskatchewan Act is long and complex, and has been repeatedly amended since its first passage but, in general, it requires, as a condition of automobile registration, that the motorist have obtained compensation insurance, for both personal injury and property, as well as $35,000 of tort liability insurance. Tort liability continues to exist, but only over and above such damages as are payable out of the compensation insurance. The compensation insurance limits are based upon a schedule of benefits patterned after workmen's compensation benefits, as recommended in the Columbia Plan and, of course, are extremely low. It is clear, therefore, that the Saskatchewan Plan is not primarily designed to reduce court litigation, but is merely designed to provide a system of minimum compensation for those persons hurt in automobile accidents under such circumstances that they would not be able to obtain recovery at all on the basis of tort liability. The Saskatchewan Plan provides for the writing of insurance by a governmental insurance organization called the Saskatchewan Government Insurance Office, or SGIO. Thus the private automobile insurance industry has been largely eliminated in Saskatchewan.

The implementation and operation of the Saskatchewan Plan has few, if any, implications in regard to the automobile insurance reform movement in the United States. It has "worked" to the extent that it has functioned smoothly, that the minimum "workmen's compensation" type payments have been made to all the victims, and that there has not been an overindulgence in automobile accident litigation under this scheme. It has certainly not worked at all in regard to other factors: it has not provided any options whatever to motorists in the allocation of their personal resources; it does not distinguish, in its compulsory features, between the responsible and irresponsible motorist, either in regard to driving characteristics or financial ability to meet potential losses; it has not provided any method of encouraging safer highway design, automobile design, or automobile operation; and it contains no features designed to further the goals of individually-tailored full compensation for automobile accident victims injured as the result of the culpable behavior of another.

Again in the 1950's, a period which saw the stirrings of a great many governmental and other reform groups in the United States, the American branch of the automobile insurance reform movement sprang back to life. In 1954, Professor Albert A. Ehrenzweig of the University of California Law School published a book proposing a system of automobile accident compensation insurance patterned, once again, closely after the system initially presented in the Columbia Report. Professor Ehrenzweig's compensation system revolved around the creation of a new type of automobile insurance called "full aid insurance," under which benefits would be provided for automobile insurance victims without regard to the principles of negligence and tort liability, under a schedule of payments similar to that found in workmen's compensation insurance, much like the Columbia Plan. Motorists obtaining this "full aid insurance" would be exempted from tort liability, at least ot the extent of the insurance benefits payable under the full aid insurance policy, so that their victims would look to the insurance policy for compensation. The benefits were not, of course, individually tailored to the victim, nor was any compensation for general damages provided, but presumably these additional damages could be compensated under the traditional tort law system.

Perhaps the outstanding feature of Professor Ehrenzweig's proposal was that it recognized the importance of continuing to provide a degree of individual freedom and responsibility for American motorists; the insurance included in the proposal was voluntary rather than compulsory. A great many inducements to purchase the insurance were included in the proposal, however, including the exemption from common law liability under the insurance coverages, the expected lower premiums resulting from the elimination of some of the costs of adjusting claims, and adoption of the principles incorporated in traditional financial responsibility legislation. Recognizing the problem of the uninsured motorist under such financial responsibility legislation as a social problem, Ehrenzweig proposed an "uncompensated-injury fund" to provide full aid insurance benefits to those victims without such a policy to which to turn. This fund was to be built up and replenished from the proceeds from common law rights of action against third persons not having the "full aid insurance" exempting them from tort liability, from the proceeds of certain fines to be levied against those motorists found guilty of criminal negligence (called "tort fines"), and from general tax revenues.

Several of the deficiencies in Professor Ehrenzweig's proposal are obvious, and perhaps the most important shortcoming was his presentation of the plan as an idea rather than as a polished and completed legislative proposal. The plan stimulated great interest however, and probably as a result of its realistic assessment of the importance of traditional political and economic freedoms to the American citizenry, the plan served to provide an additional base of consideration upon which all future proposals should be built.

In 1958, however, Professor Leon Green of the University of Texas published a book proposing another system of reform in this area of the law. Professor Green's proposal, apparently in recognition of the importance of individually tailored damages in the American jurisprudential scheme, avoided the "workmen's compensation" type benefit schedule which had served as a basis of recovery under the Columbia Plan, the Saskatchewan Plan, and Professor Ehrenzweig's proposal. Damages would be determined under the ordinary laws of damages, in ordinary court trials if necessary.

The victim still stood to lose, however, under Green's proposal in comparison with his traditional rights under tort liability. Only "out-of-pocket" losses would be covered, with absolutely no provision for general damages, and all of the innocent victims' ordinary tort law remedies would be abrogated. The tort law system of negligence liability was entirely eliminated under this proposal, and a victim was left with his rights under the insurance policies, and no other. In addition, the Green proposal called for universally compelled insurance coverage. Every motorist regardless of individual characteristics or circumstances, as a requirement of registering an automobile, would be required to show evidence of insurance coverage, with the concomitant misallocation of the cost of automobile accidents.

Green's proposal met with wide acceptance, but like most

of the other preceding proposals it was never seriously considered for adoption as law. Despite the merit of Green's general approach to the damages problem, not only did his plan suffer the
obvious difficulties of any proposal including compulsory loss insurance, eliminating all general damages, and entirely eliminating tort law from the applicability but, once again, it was presented in a very sketchy form, more as an idea than as a con-
crete legislative proposal.

The realization that the measure of the victims' damages
was of vital importance was also obvious in the proposal by Professors Clarence Morris and James Paul, of the University of
Pennsylvania Law School, in their article in 1962, published in
Pennsylvania Law Review, and presenting another new plan. Professors Morris and Paul accurately pinpointed and emphasized the
fact that under the traditional system of automobile accident reparations, small and middle-sized cases, in terms of damages,
were fully compensated, or nearly so (including general damages),
but that very large cases tended to be frequently and grievously
under-compensated. Drawing the line in relation to very large
cases at $800 or uncompensated medical expenses and earning
losses, the professors proposed a fund to reimburse expenses
incurred above that limit. The fund would not provide full, individually tailored compensation, as did the traditional system,
but it would provide substantial compensation (85%, with certain
other limits) of certain out-of-pocket (actual medical expenses
and earnings loss) damages. Half a loaf, they reasoned, in these
cases is better than none.

The exact nature of the fund was not precisely described in
the article, but it was suggested that the fund might be either
government-supported by some form of tax on motoring, or pri-
vately-supported based upon a surcharge included in all automobile insurance premiums.

In recognition of the fact that establishment of such a fund
would create additional financial burdens upon motorists, the
authors seized upon the general damages, often viewed as over-
compensation, in the smaller cases as source of monies to finance
the proposal. General damages in these smaller cases, because
of the less disastrous overall economic consequences of the out-
of-pocket losses incurred in such cases, have generally been
viewed by automobile insurance reformers as overly generous,

and such small claims, therefore, as have been previously mentioned, have come to be recognized as "nuisance claims." In order to reduce the value of such nuisance claims, thereby foregoing full compensation in the small claims in order to achieve the greater social good of providing some minimum out-of-pocket compensation for the larger claims, Professors Morris and Paul proposed that all general damages should be barred in cases in which the out-of-pocket expenses total less than $800, that no damages in any cases by payable to the extent that compensation might be available from some collateral source, and that the system of attorneys fees for such claims be changed.

The proposal of Professors Morris and Paul is outstanding in several regards. Not only does it provide for individually tailored damages, and not only is it based upon a system of voluntary insurance with certain inducements to participate, both vital recognitions of the importance of traditional American individual liberties, but it also is designed specifically to deal with what is probably the most serious failing in the traditional reparations system, i.e., that victims with large catastrophic losses frequently go largely uncompensated. Furthermore, within limits, their proposal seems designed to provide a reasonable allocation of the costs of automobile activity.

Bearing in mind the above outstanding characteristics of their proposal, most particularly the fact that it is addressed directly to the most serious of the difficulties with the traditional system, it is perhaps surprising that their proposal did not have a more pervasive affect upon the automobile insurance reform movement than has in fact been the case. Like some of the earlier proposals, this one was presented in very brief form, not fleshed out with the details which would be necessary for legislative implementation, and this sketchiness undoubtedly served as a limiting influence upon the pervasiveness of the proposal. Probably more important, however, is the very reasonableness of the plan itself. In recognizing the importance of traditional American freedom, and thereby retaining a system of voluntary insurance, while at the same time calling for certain changes which would create an additional burden upon some of the vested interest in regard to the present system, Professors Morris and Paul fashioned a plan which was doubtless limited by its own reasonableness. Representatives of vested interests, confident at the time that any change at all could be avoided, obviously had no reason to rush to the support of this proposal. Neither, on the other hand, did the bulk of automobile insurance "reformers" who were dogmatically committed to the principle of universal compulsion as a political principle. It seems likely that the Morris and Paul proposal, if it were being presented today, would probably be widely accepted by many parties on the automobile insurance reform scene, excepting the hidebound "reformers." Indeed, some of the most widely accepted and reasonable of the more modern proposals are based upon principles not greatly unlike those espoused in the Morris and Paul proposal of ten years ago.

Early in 1965, the State Bar of California, through a "Special Committee on Personal Injury Claims," published a proposal once again calling for universally compelled purchase of automobile accident compensation insurance. The proposal, in addition, provided for purchase (also universally compelled) of traditional liability insurance and automobile medical payments insurance. With these exceptions, the existing reparations system was to remain intact. The proposal was subject to a great many questions and reservations, even among its own committee membership, and like the earlier proposals discussed, was presented in very general form. Because of the stir which it created, however, focusing the automobile insurance reform movement once again upon universal compulsion, the California proposal served to abrogate the effect of the vestiges of influence of the Morris and Paul approach.

Later in 1965, a book was published which was destined to become the most important contribution to the automobile insurance reform movement since the Columbia Report, and the second milestone in that movement. That book, _Basic Protection for the Traffic Victim_, by Professor Robert E. Keeton of Harvard University Law School and Jeffrey O'Connell of the Law School of the University of Illinois, was generally a restatement and re-embodiment of the principles common to most of the earlier reform efforts, denying full compensation to those victims injured as a result of the negligence of others, in favor of partial compensation not only to innocent victims but to guilty victims as well, through the medium of universally compelled compensation insurance. The first part of that book consists of comprehensive examination of the traditional system of automobile accident reparations, the problems therewith, and previous proposals for reform, some of which have been discussed here.

The second half of the book presented the authors' proposal destined to become nationally known as "the Keeton-O'Connell Plan," consisting, as has been mentioned, of universally compelled automobile compensation insurance. Any motorist holding an insurance policy under this plan (i.e., all motorists, if the plan works as intended) would be released from responsibility under the traditional principles of negligence, for any injuries inflicted by him resulting in damages up to $10,000, or in the case of general damages, $5,000. The victim, in such a case, would recover certain elements of his damage, without regard to traditional principles of fault or liability, from an insurance company, and would forego other elements of his damages entirely. Above the $10,000 limit, the traditional reparations system would continue to operate as it has in the past.

The outstanding characteristics of this proposal are not the elements outlined, for these are neither new nor original. The outstanding quality of the Keeton-O'Connell proposal was the inclusion of proposed implementing legislation, with commentary. In the process of fleshing out the proposal, Professors Keeton and O'Connell met and dealt with a great many of the technical but important problems arising in the implementation of any system of comprehensive automobile insurance reform. The plan also incorporated, through its very comprehensiveness, a great many of the technical reforms urged by earlier writers (periodic payment of damages, e.g.) not comprehensively worked into previous reform proposals but meeting with almost universal acceptance.

The Keeton-O'Connell Proposal, possibly because of the atmosphere and history of the automobile insurance movement in which it was generated, had a great immediate and far reaching affect upon the automobile insurance reform movement. The plan was almost immediately introduced into the Massachusetts legislature, and was considered as potential legislation all across the country. Initial debates concerning the plan consisted of almost no discussion whatever concerning the jurisprudential and philosophical bases of the plan or of the effect which its implementation would have upon the lives and rights of American citizens, but rather upon its costs. The Keeton and O'Connell proposal, with the prediction that the average motorist automobile insurance premiums would be greatly reduced as a result of their plan. The reduction was expected to result partly from the fact that full compensation was to be denied victims with out-of-pocket losses less than $10,000 or general damages of $5,000, therefore reducing insurance company payout for this class of claims, and partly from an expected reduction in litigation under their proposal. The expected reduction in litigation would not have any direct effect upon payout, of course, but the assumption was that victims would be satisfied with lower payments for their losses because they would not have to pay any legal fees.

The battle over the Keeton-O'Connell plan raged for sometime, limited primarily to its cost aspects, in the process failing of passage in the Massachusetts Legislature. In the months that followed, the Keeton-O'Connell automobile insurance reform proposal was perhaps the single most popular subject of articles editorials and discussion in business, insurance and legal journals across the country, as well as at conventions, seminars, and in private conversations concerned with this area of American life. Untold numbers of proposals and counter-proposals sprang to life as the discussion broadened from the mere cost aspect of the proposal to technical implementation and feasibility, and finally including its philosophical and jurisprudential basis.

At present, a good deal (but certainly not all) of the furor generated by the Keeton-O'Connell proposal has died down, partly because the entire issue has become almost hopelessly buried under the mass of discussion and literature generated by the controversy. Well over 100 proposals and counter-proposals, compatible and incompatible with the Keeton-O'Connell proposal, have been presented. Many of these proposals are relatively complete (though very few of them are as complete as the Keeton-O'Connell plan) and many of them consist of only a single thrust in the attack upon alleged deficiencies in the present system, with others filling in the entire range in-between. One entire publication is devoted to nothing more than the enumeration and outlining of the various proposals.

The Keeton-O'Connell Proposal, reintroduced into the Massachusetts legislature on occasion, in various forms, was finally enacted in that state in 1970, in greatly modified form. The philosophical and jurisprudential difficulties with the plan were of little moment in Massachusetts, where universal compulsion in this area of the law has existed since 1927, and the proposal which became law in that state differs from its progenitor in certain technical details, and in the limits of the insurance coverage and tort liability exemption provided; not in its basic approach to the problem.

The automobile reform act implemented in Massachusetts provides that the compensation insurance in the amount of at least $2,000 is compulsory upon all motorists wishing to register motor vehicles. The compensation insurance policy for any particular registered automobile provides coverage for any person injured while riding in that automobile, or any person injured as a result of that automobile's operation in the event that such a victim is not covered by another policy insuring him in regard to an auto- mobile in which he was riding at the time of the injury.

The insurance benefits consist of payment of medical ex- penses, a portion of lost wages not otherwise compensated, and actual payments for certain non-income producing services per- formed by others on behalf of the injured person. (Property dam- age losses, it might be emphasized, are not included at all under the plan, so they are not paid under the insurance scheme but may still be recovered through the traditional tort liability ma- chinery.) No other damages resulting from personal injuries may be recovered, either under the insurance policy or, as a result of the exemption from tort liability, through the traditional prin- ciples of reparations. Such damages must be absorbed by the victim.

The limit of benefits payable is $2,000. Damages in excess of this figure may be recovered through optional insurance, if purchased, just as under the traditional reparations system, or through the traditional system of tort liability. In the event that reasonable and necessary medical expenses exceed $500, general damages, even though not recoverable under the insurance bene- fits, may be sought through the traditional tort liability system.

The authors of the Keeton-O'Connell Proposal have claimed that the compulsory compensation insurance scheme adopted in Massachusetts represents a great deviation from their original proposals, and it would seem that inasmuch as the philosophical base of universal compulsion, in Massachusetts predates the

introduction of their plan and in view of the vast technical differences between the plan as implemented and their original proposal, there is merit in that position. Nonetheless, the adoption
of the compensation insurance plan in Massachusetts must stand
as the high water mark of the Keeton-O'Connell proposal. In
subsequent legislative consideration across the country, the Keeton-O'Connell proposal seems to have been replaced by a new
and more moderate approach.

That new approach, however, has not deterred the forces
of those reformers in favor of various forms of universally compulsory compensation insurance. Throughout 1970 the United
States Department of Transportation was engaged in a massive
study of the automobile accident reparations system, and a number of volumes were published containing the findings and reports
generated by that study. Not surprisingly, bearing in mind that
the entire study was the result of the reform movement, the out-
come of the D.O.T. study appears to be an overall adoption of
the principle of universally compulsory compensation insurance.
Such a plan, in appropriate legislative detail is being prepared
for the D.O.T. by a committee of the National Council of Comm-
issioners of Uniform State Laws (N.C.C.U.S.A.), to be ready in
December 1971. Professor Keeton is a consulting member of that
committee.

The usual function of that group (N.C.C.U.S.A.) is the promulgation of legislation appropriate for implementation in all
states, with the announced goal of attaining uniformity in state
laws. Undoubtedly the completion of the drafting the bill for the
D.O.T. by the committee will be followed by the drafting of a
bill for consideration for such promulgation. Such promulgation
would be of great importance, perhaps of the same note as the
Columbia Report and Basic Protection for the Traffic Victim, and
would hopefully reflect consideration of the more reasonable and
moderate approach, based upon specific solutions to specific
problems, evident in some of the more recent legislative and
other proposals.

The years following the publication of Keeton and O'Connell's
Basic Protection for the Traffic Victim, have seen some deempha-
sis of the importance of the movement towards compulsory compensation insurance, with all of its ramifications, and the birth
and growth of a new automobile insurance reform movement,

evidenced by various types of proposals characterized by provisions selectively and specifically designed to achieve a constructive attack upon the weaknesses of the traditional reparations system within a framework of as little substantive change from that system as possible. In March 1969, for example, Preferred Risk Mutual Automobile Insurance Company of Des Moines, Iowa, introduced, without a great deal of national fanfare, the first active no-fault automobile insurance program in the nation. The policy issued by Preferred Risk Mutual Insurance Company contained, as an integral part which could be removed from the automobile liability policy only at the express request of the policyholder, language providing for immediate payment of medical expenses and lost wages, payable without regard to fault, for all parties normally eligible for traditional "medical payments" insurance. The program was designed to eliminate the problems of delay in payment as explained previously, as well as providing some measure of recovery concerning loss of earnings, previously unavailable, for victims unable to recover under the traditional principles of tort liability. All indications based upon early experience with this plan, indicate that it has been and will continue to be quite successful, both for the policyholders and for the issuing company.

In March 1971, a proposal typifying the approach of this "new wave" in the automobile insurance reform movement, in complete form for legislative enactment (as opposed to the insurance company unilateral action in the previous case), was put forth by the Illinois Department of Insurance, under Governor Richard B. Ogilvie. This proposal, known as the Illinois Plan, would require that every automobile liability policy issued within the state contain language providing certain compensation insurance benefits, including medical, hospital and funeral benefits, income continuation benefits, and loss of services benefits. These benefits would be available to the same parties who would be eligible for traditional medical payments coverage, as well as to pedestrians, as under the Keeton O'Connell Plan. These benefits were to be payable without regard to fault, promptly, and on a periodic basis where losses could be reasonably expected to extend beyond a 30-day period.

In addition to these basic provisions, the policyholder would have available to him, on an optional basis, additional no-fault coverage which would greatly expand the extent of the benefits. In order to preserve the allocation of costs, shifting the burden to those drivers responsible for the accident, subrogation of claims was expressly continued, with the potentiality of excess litigation reduced by compulsory arbitration in the case of subrogation claims.

Governor Ogilvie's proposal also provided for court supervised mandatory arbitration in the case of all automobile injury cases, with rights to a trial de novo upon the motion of either party. General damages were continued, but limited to 50% of the first $500 of medical expenses and 100% of the excess over $500.

Certain similarities and certain dissimilarities can instantly be seen to exist between the automobile insurance reform movement as typified by the Columbia Report and the Keeton-O'Connell proposal, and as more recently presented in Governor Ogilvie's "Illinois Plan." All of the proposals have recognized the seriousness of uncompensated victims with losses of catastrophic proportions, and have recognized that certain basic economic needs should be capable of being met on a compensatory basis, without regard to fault. In both cases, the possibility of effecting savings in insurance premiums through the reasonable limitations of the right to recover general damages in less serious cases is recognized. All such proposals have recognized the importance of the implementation of a system of prompt periodic payment of losses, and of administrative systems capable of providing adjudication of automobile accident claims in those jurisdictions where court congestion and delay is a serious problem.

It is precisely in regard to such problems as these that the necessity for the distinction between the types of problems being attacked by automobile insurance reforms becomes vitally important. These problems are administrative in nature, resulting from certain deficiencies in the operation of the traditional system, and are therefore properly subject to "reform." The difficulty with the Keeton-O'Connell proposal and its similar predecessors and followers is that these proposals do not limit themselves to such reforms, but rather constitute a concerted attack upon the very basis of American justice as incorporated in the traditional system of automobile reparations. Such an approach is avoided in legislation as typified by the Illinois Plan (even though that plan, too, has its deficiencies, in that it does not represent a wholly comprehensive attack upon both the causes and the results of difficulties with the traditional approach).

Chapter Three

AN ORDERING OF PRIORITIES

It is deceptively easy, spurred on by simplistic, rather than meaningful, idealism, to enumerate an impressive list of goals or criteria for an effective automobile accident reparation system. Such a utopian exposition can result almost accidentally from an uncritical examination of the needs of society on any level. Examples of such criteria which have been suggested for an automobile insurance system are: "it should compensate all victims," "it should pay high benefits," "it should have low premiums," "it should be reliable," and "it should be stable." Other suggestions in this same vein might be: "it should be in the best of American tradition," "it should meet the public needs," or "it should be good."

Such a listing makes good copy, but is unfortunately not very helpful in any realistic way in trying to construct, analyze or evaluate an automobile insurance system. There can be no doubt that what we want is a "good" system, but it is either naivete or presumption to attempt to assert with any confidence what is objectively "good." Subjective notions of the "public good" have time and again throughout history proven inimical to American principles of self-determination.

Some of the supposed criteria are meaningless. To say that a system should be "good," that it should be "stable," that it should be "efficient" or that it should be "fair," is misleading and self-serving, inasmuch as these are emotionally laden, subjective and imprecise terms. Such adjectives as these are not values to be served, but comparative evaluations based upon subjective opinion.

The unfaced fact in the dialogue concerning the automobile insurance system is that for every value included, in the final analysis, opposing values must be foregone. Even such innocent values as "efficiency" and "fairness" are meaningless until effectuated by specific implementations involving hard choices between conflicting values.

If, for instance, we are to say that a system should pay all victims, and that it should pay high benefits, and that it should have low premiums, we have in the entirety said nothing capable of realistic implementation. The concept of paying all victims, with high benefits, while charging low premiums, is so internally conflicting that it obviously cannot be put into practice in any absolute sense. To the contrary, a realistic approach must be founded upon an examination of the continuum on the scale from low premiums and low benefits to high premiums and high benefits, with a view towards determining where the line should be drawn. High benefits and low premiums may only appear to be compatible as the result of a collateral confusing of the issues, and ultimately they are directly opposed to one another and cannot be both fully served as values in the same system. Rather, they must be "accommodated."

Other standards which might be listed as criteria of a good system, while not so directly opposed as "high benefits and low premiums," are nonetheless indirectly opposed, in that full implementation of these criteria in coordination is impossible. It is likely that any two criteria which could be conceived would conflict if pushed to the ultimate. What needs to be undertaken, therefore, when attempting to construct the criteria of a good system, is an objective analysis of all the possible criteria, with an understanding and full realization of the conflicts involved between and among the various possibilities.

All that can be done, then, is to list the issues involved, as comprehensively as possible, and choose <u>priorities</u>. The resultant list of priorities must include recognition of the conflicts and must be based upon a realistic choice among <u>all</u> the values involved. It must allocate priorities to conflicting values only in realistic proportions, and it must ultimately bear the test of rational inquiry. Only by such consideration of the criteria applicable to the automobile insurance system, and their relative priorities, can the degree to which and the direction in which reform should proceed be determined. None of the following values can be followed absolutely; the conflicts between the various goals cannot be avoided.

.Provide Universal Compensation

This criteria represents a need for some improvement upon

the present system. The existing system operates in such a manner that nearly all victims (eighty to ninety percent) receive some form of compensation, but universal compensation would require some sort of change.

.Provide Full Individually-Tailored Compensation Wherever Possible

Full, individually-tailored, compensation is specifically provided in the present system, though limited to those individuals who have valid tort claims. Thus this criteria would require a change in the system only if it were separately determined that all automobile accident victims should receive equal benefits.

.Provide Prompt Compensation

The present system may, under some circumstances, be somewhat deficient in the area of providing prompt compensation. Compensation should be prompt. The factors in the operation of the present system which mitigate against prompt payments to victims by liability carriers have been previously examined. One clear change which might be indicated in this regard would be some alteration of the rule providing for the admissability of advance payments as evidence tending to prove liability in a subjective tort suit.

.Provide Periodic Compensation

Optimally, payments should be periodic as well as prompt. In the case of wage loss, for example, the wages lost were likely to have been periodically paid, and replacement of this loss with a lump-sum judgment, while in the best tradition of American jurisprudence, places an undue burden upon the recipient of the award. The victim may need his medical expenses and wage losses to be compensated as accrued.

.Morally Appropriate Allocation of Costs

The practical allocation of costs as under the present system is morally acceptable to the American public. The tort system is based upon fault, and there is no evidence that the American public has lost faith in this system as a morally appropriate basis for the allocation of cost. Even to the extent that this particular allocation of costs is defeated by the liability insurance system, the classification plans inherent in that system serve to re-establish the morality of the cost as allocated, inasmuch as high risk drivers will pay high premiums and low risk drivers will pay low premiums.

.Rational Allocation of Cost

Morally appropriate cost allocations are also rationally appropriate allocations, but socially rational allocation of cost has greater ramifications. The severe limitations upon the classification plan mitigate against the <u>completely</u> effective allocation of costs on a rational basis. Furthermore, classification plans as applied through the first-party insurance mechanism are even less effective than those applied through the liability insurance mechanism. Rational allocation of costs would require that cost be placed proportionately with the degree of risk, whether the risk is a liability or a direct insurance risk. In order to achieve this goal, the present system need not be changed, but it must be improved.

.Improved Safety by Inducing Safe Driving

It has been previously demonstrated that the present system serves as a complement to the criminal law system. As designed, the system, through the operation of deterrents, tends to discourage negligent driving. There can be little doubt that the classification plan and its attendant threat of increase in insurance rates and possible suspension of coverage operates as a strong deterrent to negligent driving.

.Encourage Private Enterprise and American Traditions

No change in the system is needed in order to achieve this goal, and radical change might work to the opposite effect.

.Lower the Cost of the System Through Efficiency

The cost of the present system is not unreasonable when the treble nature and function (tort claim protection, deterrence of negligent behavior, and first-party coverage) of the present system are considered. At the same time, the high cost of automobile insurance has created some dissatisfaction among the American public. To remove the dissatisfaction, costs attributable to inefficiency in the system need to be eliminated. The lowest possible premium commensurate with the more important goals listed above should be achieved to whatever degree possible. Clearly some mechanisms designed to encourage efficiency, and therefore lower costs, should be incorporated into the present system.

.Provide Evolutionary Reform

Improvements in the present system, as indicated by the priorities above, are required. These changes should be provided for in such a manner that the reform in the system is evolutionary in nature. Unreasoned and unnecessary changes in any system serve to generate crosscurrents of purpose. Change provides problems which are frequently unmeasurable, unrecognizable and not prospectively anticipated or solved. Change should be gradual. Adjustments generated by the change must be capable of being measured and evaluated at each level prior to additional steps in the change process.

.Protect Against Social and Economic Upheaval

Any system sanctioned by society generates those individuals or groups who develop a great dependence upon the system. These individuals or groups therefore develop a vested interest in the continuation of the system, and their own personal welfare depends upon the system's continued existence. Such vested interests create two entirely opposite considerations when change is considered. First, it must be realized that these vested interests exist, and that certain objections to change may be generated simply as a result of that vested interest. Such objections to change need to be scrutinized, so that the status quo is not

preserved simply as a servant to the vested interest, when change
would better serve the needs of society. On the other hand, these
vested interests often represent a friendly force in our society.
The entire stability of society depends upon protecting individuals in their valid vested interests, so that they may order their
lives and plan accordingly. Violent social upheaval may result,
unnecessarily, if vested interests are eliminated wholesale,
without allowance for the lives, investments and plans of the individuals involved. Such social upheaval can be softened if change
is gradual.

.Spur Improvement in Automobile, Highway, and Related Design

The present system has partially failed in spurring improvement in automobile and highway design. The present system has begun to supply some impetus in this direction through
the classification rating plan of liability insurance policies whereby certain automobiles may be rated higher than others; but such
a classification plan is in its infancy. It is obvious that the allocation of costs under the system needs to be improved. The
extra risk presented by poorly designed automobiles and highways
must be taken into account. In reference to highways, this variable is considered somewhat in the geographical classifications
under rating systems, but once again the operation of the system in this regard is somewhat imprecise and unreliable at this
time.

Encourage Social Change

The insurance industry's obligation to encourage social
change must not be allowed to become distorted as a result of
semantics. Any force in our society has an obligation to perform its functions in the most satisfactory manner possible, and
the improvements which become necessary and possible as the
results of technical or sociological progress may result in some
incidental social change. This obligation of improved perform-
ance, however, should be limited in operation to that social
change which is necessary to further and improve the operation
of the system, not social change which might be considered by

some to be independently desirable.

.Provide Objective Equality in Rates

There is obviously some merit in the provision of objective equality. A great deal of the apparent merit of such a proposal, however, results merely from the simplistic view inherent in the thought itself, rather than from an evaluation of the actual operation of such a system. Equality of rates, on an objective scale, is actually a manifestation of <u>inequality</u> of the individual's risk-premium ratio. There is no equality in charging a high-risk driver the same insurance premium as a low-risk driver.

.Provide Objective Equality in Benefits

The same objections bear upon objective equality of benefits as upon objective equality in rates. There is no equality in providing the same benefit for the loss of the right arm of a baseball pitcher as for the right arm of some other, possibly quite differently situated and oriented victim. In either case, equal rates or equal benefits may or may not be appropriate, but "equality" is an elusive and simplistic concept.

.Follow the Lead of Other Nations or Improve Their Systems

It has been widely suggested that other nations, particularly other Western nations, have insurance systems after which we could well pattern our American law. Undoubtedly the operation of these systems can serve as valuable sociological input in any consideration of how our system should change. At the same time, we must not lose sight of the fact that the ordering of priorities in these other nations may differ greatly from the ordering of priorities traditional in America. These other nations do not always have a tradition of individual freedom of choice and action such as ours, and they may place no great emphasis upon such freedom. Therefore, it is clear that, to the extent to which an individual subjectively accepts another nation's different ordering of pirorities, he may approve of the automobile insurance system as it has evolved in these other countries. This does not mean, of course, that such systems would be applicable in the

United States except to the extent that the American public would be willing to accept the reordering of priorities which form the background for the system.

.Encourage the Growth and Function of Government

In recent years there has been a considerable trend to encourage the growth and function of government, supposedly upon the basis that government is more pure in its motives than are the instrumentalities of private enterprise. This trend has been evident in a number of automobile insurance proposals. However, this particular trend, is directly at odds with the traditional American goal of encouraging private enterprise, and so should not be served by the automobile accident reparations systems to the extent of creating conflict.

.Providing for Adherence to Individual Notions of Good

This is a "value" which in its ramifications has been put forth extensively in supporting various proposals in the automobile insurance area. It would clearly appear to be a value which should be positively avoided.

It is intended that other goals frequently mentioned but not individually listed are meant to be included within the various headings above. It is hoped that the above listing, construed broadly, fairly well represents the issues which have been widely discussed as possible criteria for a new insurance law system Obviously, such meaningless criteria as "good," "reliable," and similar subjective terms of praise have been omitted.

The above goals have been listed in the order of priority upon which the Multiple Benefits Plan is based, as criteria which should be met by an automobile insurance system. That this ranking of priorities is subjective cannot be denied, and reasonable men may differ in ranking priorities. The Multiple Benefits Plan must stand or fall on this base, however, which is at least the result of one evaluation of American jurisprudence, American tradition and the specific automobile accident needs which must be met. In the place of "provide forced adherence to individual notions of public good," the criteria which is--

whether or not admittedly--frequently given top priority in an-
alyzing such systems, the above order of priorities addresses
itself, hopefully objectively, to the individual weaknesses and
problems in the present automobile reparation system, in an
attempt to recognize the needs presented by those problems.
Under this ranking of priorities, if our entire present system
needs to be scrapped in order to serve the needs, so be it. But
the system should not be scrapped as a goal in itself, independently of the needs of the public.

In this regard, it is necessary that we take a good hard look
at the function of the insurance industry and modern American
society. Probably no other instrumentality in our country, short
of the government itself, is in a position to have a greater impact as a social motivating force upon our American traditions
and our American way of life than the insurance industry. The
influence of this industry is not only economically powerful, but
socially pervasive.

Because of this vast power, it must be the function of the
insurance industry to serve the needs of the American society.
The industry must move quickly and responsively, much more
so than in the past, to meet the needs of insurees, and to adjust
the systems with which it works in order to achieve those appropriate goals. Concurrently, also because of its vast power, the
industry must balk at being used as a tool by social planners or
others who would use the power of the industry to force their
particular individual notions of "the public good" upon the American society. The problems of our society cry out for solution;
but the individuals in our society do not cry out for control, for
being told how to live, for being told how to allocate their resources.

It should be the mission of the insurance industry, through
the judicious application of the power at its disposal, to move into the problem areas in society and address itself to the needs in
those areas, approaching those needs definitively rather than
with the "big guns." Massive, unfounded changes in the insurance industry may bring about such great and unanticipated changes
in our American way of life, because of the influence of the industry, that time-honored traditions may be swept aside thought-
lessly in the rush to cure problems which, when compared with
the havoc wrought by the misguided efforts to effect their cure,

may ultimately prove not to have been so great after all.

The mission of the insurance industry, in the automobile reparations system, is to address itself to meeting the needs which exist, and to apply all of its resources to whatever extent is necessary in order to meet those needs. No less will suffice to solve the problems, and no more can be tolerated.

Chapter Four

THE ISSUE OF COMPULSORY INSURANCE

Whether or not automobile insurance should be made compulsory has been, perhaps, the most controversial issue in the entire discussion concerning the possibilities of reform of the automobile insurance industry. Three of our states, New York, Massachusetts, and North Carolina, have made <u>liability</u> insurance compulsory, Massachusetts in 1927 and the other two states more recently; throughout these years, other states have resisted compulsory insurance. The controversy rages today perhaps more strongly than ever before, as academicians continue to put forth insurance proposals calling for compulsory insurance. Occasionally a legislature considers such a proposal, but usually the insurance industry and the public oppose such proposals.

The rationale for compulsory insurance could not be simpler. In the search for financial responsibility on the part of motorists - realizing that financial responsibility can nearly always be equated with automobile liability insurance - any procedure which promises to guarantee a more widespread coverage of motorists by that liability insurance is said to be a "good" thing.

The assumption, however, that compulsory insurance results in a higher percentage of motorists being insured, has not gone unchallenged. Indeed, research reveals that the three states of our country which have enacted compulsory insurance laws, although <u>among</u> those states with the highest percentage of insurance coverage, do not "lead the field" in that regard. As a matter of fact, other states, without compulsory insurance, have achieved higher percentages of insured motorists without legislatively compelling all motorists by law to buy these policies. It is clear, at least, that compulsory insurance requirements have failed in their attempt to force all motorists to buy liability insurance; not <u>all</u> motorists do so, even when the law provides penalties for the failure to comply.

All of the other states in our country have enacted financial responsibility laws which operate in such a manner as to make purchase of automobile liability insurance (or an appropriate cash bond) compulsory on the part of those individuals who present demonstratively higher risks in regard to their driving of a motor vehicle. This type of compulsion has been termed "selective compulsion, "as compared with the "universal compulsion" of the other procedure. The standards for so classifying such motorists differ from state to state, but generally involve a failure to satisfy a tort judgment resulting from a previous automobile accident.

Social Desirability of Compulsion

The moral and political principle of financial responsibility laws, is that compulsion, as such, is basically opposed to our traditional American way of life and should be imposed only when and as absolutely necessary. Generally speaking, their proponents reason, an individual in America should be allowed to allocate his private resources according to his own decisions, and the allocation of those resources should not be forced upon him by legislative fiat. To the extent to which governmental bodies have been empowered to undertake certain activities for the public good they may, of course, finance these activities through the power of taxation, but the taxation power cannot be compared to compelling the purchase of compulsory liability insurance. This issue, however, has been somewhat confused in some quarters, as will be discussed below.

It is clear that financial responsibility laws represent an implementation of the "first bite rule" in the automobile accident context. This rule is so titled because it has been extended from the ancient and continuing doctrine that an individual who harbors a dog without knowledge that the dog has a tendency to be vicious cannot be held liable if the dog in a fit of aberrational behavior bites someone. After the "first bite," however, the keeper of the dog is deemed to be on notice of the dog's tendency toward viciousness, and can be held liable for any future vicious behavior of the animal. The application of this principle in our financial responsibility legislation is clear. Those individuals who have not been involved in an accident which was their fault, and afterwards failed to satisfy a judgment against them, have not demonstrated any behavior which would indicate that they should have their traditional American right of private determination of allocation of resources taken from them, and are therefore not required to provide evidence of financial responsibility. Only after such an occurrence can these individuals be clearly labeled as individuals presenting a risk of financial irresponsibility and, to the extent to which they wish to continue operating on the highways, be required to give evidence that they will be financially responsible in the event of future accidents resulting from their negligence.

Because there are certain individuals who will exercise their right to allocation of resources in such a manner as to in fact remain financially insolvent and uninsured, and at the same time operate their vehicles in such a manner that they may cause an accident and be found to be at fault, it is possible that some victims of automobile accidents may have enforceable tort claims and receive judgments, only to find that these judgments are unenforceable against the defendant. This will occur if defendant is both judgment-proof and without liability insurance coverage.

Financial responsibility laws are designed to prevent a second example of such a circumstance being precipitated by an individual who, by failing to satisfy a tort judgment resulting from a previous automobile accident, has shown that he cannot be trusted in this regard. But the "first bite" will result in the initial judgment against such motorists being unenforceable against them.

Clearly individual freedom has its costs. In the case of financial responsibility laws the cost of continuing the freedom of individuals to determine by their own private wills how they will allocate their resources may result in uncompensated victims with unsatisfied judgments, unless some other machinery or instrumentality is instituted in order to solve this problem.

One such instrumentality is uninsured motorist protection. Any individual, unless unable to obtain such interest on the voluntary market because of his own driving characteristics, may obtain uninsured motorist protection at a nominal fee, as an adjunct portion of his automobile insurance package. For those individuals who decline (or are unable) to purchase uninsured motorist protection, the problem of unsatisfied judgments has been solved in some jurisdictions by the creation of an unsatisfied judgment fund. (See supa p.54) The Assigned Liability Claims Plan of the Multiple Benefits Plan serves this same function without the creation of the fund and its attendant bureaucracy.

<u>Constitutional Considerations</u>

In addition, there are constitutional limitations involved in compulsory insurance legislation. Of course, these constitutional limitations have been overcome in the cases of three states in which compulsory insurance legislation has been enacted, but it is notable that in all three of those states the compulsory insurance laws refer only to liability insurance. The rationale behind such a requirement is clear, inasmuch as the driver on the highway represents, regardless of how careful he may drive, some degree of risk to other drivers on the highway. None of us, admittedly, can drive so safely that we are <u>absolutely never</u> negligent. Therefore, the constitutional limitations upon compulsory liability insurance may be overcome, but it is just as easy to solve the problem without such legislation, as has been demonstrated, through the use of unsatisfied judgment funds or assigned claim plans.

Inasmuch as both systems will work, it is a matter of comparing the relative efficiency of the two. Compulsory insurance will provide financial responsibility on the part of <u>most</u> drivers. but there will still be those drivers from whom a judgment will be uncollectible. The unsatisfied judgment fund or assigned claims plan, on the other hand, will provide for collection of judgments against any driver and therefore operates in a manner superior to compulsory automobile insurance. Indeed, the assigned claims plan could be extended to cover claims against unidentifiable individuals, such as hit and run drivers, which once again represents a coverage which would not be provided by compulsory insurance.

Not only does such a plan operate more efficiently than compulsory insurance; but it also comports more nearly with the American concept of freedom of action. True, freedom of action may be restricted in order to achieve some social good; but it is fairly clear that this freedom should not be abrogated where there are other methods, which better solve a problem, while avoiding interference with freedom of action. In any event, the primary concern is the proper allocation of costs. Under the Multiple Benefits Plan, those individuals who refuse to carry insurance will not escape the burden of their share of the cost, because of the subrogation of the assigned claims plan, and thus the costs are allocated _more_ rationally than they would be under compulsory insurance.

However, the question persists as to whether compulsory _primary_ insurance should be required. The precedent for such action is generally thought to be the enactment of workmen's compensation insurance, and the enactment of Social Security. Research indicates, however, that both of these social schemes were upheld on bases inapplicable to the automobile insurance situation.

In the case of workmen's compensation insurance, the employees were deemed, in some cases (contrary to general opinion, all workmen's compensation laws are not mandatory, and in some states - such as Iowa - the manufacturer may or may not participate in a workmen's compensation program as he sees fit) to be subject to mandatory workmen's compensation insurance. The rationale for this holding in the United States Supreme Court, however, was that the manufacturer was not being forced to allocate its own resources for this purpose at all, but that rather the manufacturer was an instrumentality which could be utilized to pass the cost of compensating the workers on to the public as part of the price of its product.

Similarly, the Social Security constitutional arguments are not applicable to the automobile insurance situation. Indeed, in the Supreme Court cases regarding the constitutionality of the Social Security laws, the contention revolved around the nature of the "tax" which was used to support the system. Clearly this "taxation" argument is not applicable to the automobile insurance situation, inasmuch as automobile insurance premiums are certainly not "taxes" payable to a government body, but are payable to companies in private industry.

As a result, the constitutional objections to compulsory first-party insurance remain. Questions of equal protection, due process, and the taking of private property are difficult and unanswered. It has been suggested that any comprehensive plan designed in our time for the furtherance of the public good would be declared constitutional despite its infringement of individual personal liberties. There may be merit in this contention, but to the extent that the contention is correct, it is a tendency by no means universally applauded.

<u>In Summary</u>

The Multiple Benefits Plan is designed to function without legislatively forcing the public to purchase the product. Market availability has been assured so that all individuals who can be determined to represent a high risk will be required to obtain insurance as a necessary part of being a high-risk driver. The Assigned Liability Claims Plan will assure that all individuals with a proper tort claim will be able to collect that claim. The subrogation principle, under that plan, will assure that individuals will have the cost shifted back to them if they are negligently responsible for injuries.

All of the individuals who obtain insurance for these reasons, will of course obtain the automatic first-party coverages as a concommitant of acquiring the desired liability coverages. As a result, it is expected that very few individuals will not be covered by both liability coverage and direct insurance coverage under the Multiple Benefits Plan. Those individuals who are not covered by liability coverage will have their claims subject to the assigned claims plan.

Some individuals may decline to purchase any of the first-party insurance coverages available to them, and subsequently suffer injuries in an accident which does not result from the provable negligence of another party. Even though statistics reveal that these individuals, unless they differ materially from accident victims in general, will be able to recover some 80-90% of the time from some other insurance source, there will inevitably be those few who have totally failed to provide, in any way at all, for their needs.

It is at this point that a value judgment must be made. To what extent will individuals, who despite all of the economic and social motivations involved in the Multiple Benefits Plan, decline to purchase insurance, represent a serious social problem. To what extent will these individuals, not being able to collect under their Dual Protection insurance, also be unable to collect a tort judgment because they were at fault (or partly at fault, or at least unable to prove fault) in an accident? To what extent will these individuals who are unable to recover under the Personal Accident Benefit of the Dual Protection Policy because they have deliberately chosen not to purchase insurance, and who are also unable to recover in tort, be also unable to recover against any of the other private insurance or governmental sources available as do some 80-90% of all accident victims? To what extent will these people who do not recover under a Dual Protection Policy because they refuse to buy insurance, and are not able to recover in tort because they cannot prove fault, be also unable to recover from other private insurance or governmental sources because they are in the 10% minority of persons who do not have such coverage? To what extent will these people be those individuals who are unable, as a result of family ties, their own personal savings, charitable contributions, or other sources, to provide for their own needs, so that they represent a burden upon society? Even to the extent that the probabilities are warped by the argument that the very same individuals are likely to fit into all these categories, must not the probabilities yet be very small?

Is it a wise or socially rational decision to require compulsory insurance, of a first-party nature, for these individuals, in the fact of the sociological, public opinion, and constitutional difficulties, in order to solve the minute problem which they represent? The answer as reflected in the Multiple Benefits Plan is obviously "no." To the extent to which individuals meet all of these criteria and thus become a burden upon society, they are clearly a social problem rather than an automobile insurance problem.

Chapter Five

A PROPOSED DUAL PROTECTION POLICY

In recognition of the new trend toward reasonable proposals designed to achieve helpful progress in the field of automobile accident reparations, within the perimeters of the goals important to American justice, there is included herein a comprehensive legislative proposal, designed to meet those goals. The proposal consists of the creation of a new form of automobile insurance policy, "Dual Protection Policy," not unlike that envisioned in the Illinois Plan or that already implemented by Preferred Risk Mutual Insurance Company, both previously described. Also included are several items of necessary and complementary collateral legislation. The benefits of the entire proposal result not so much from the individual parts of the proposal as from the interaction of these various parts in their effect upon the various goals to be achieved in automobile insurance reform.

Personal Accident Benefit

The focal point of the Multiple Benefits Plan is the Dual Protection Automobile Insurance Policy, which includes certain first-party insurance benefits in a new type of "Personal Accident Benefit" coverage. Thus every motorist purchasing automobile insurance will receive the liability insurance parts of the policy and will also automatically receive the Personal Accident Benefit. The liability and other additional coverages would be similar to those now included in the Family Automobile Policy.

The first of the automatic first-party insurance coverages in the Dual Protection Insurance Policy is "medical payments." This coverage will provide for payment of all reasonable hospital, surgical and medical expenses, covered for a period of one year from the date of the accident, up to a maximum payment of $2,000. "Reasonable medical expenses," in this context, includes "semi-private hospital room." "Reasonable funeral expense" (with an upper limit of $1,000) is also included. It is intended that this medical expense coverage will be primary coverage. However, it will be excess coverage over governmental sources, such as Medicare and Workmen's Compensation.

"Wage loss" is a second first-party insurance benefit of the Personal Accident Benefit coverage. The direct insurance benefit will be 80% of current wages at the time of the accident, up to a maximum of $750 a month. The 80% figure is a presumption only, based upon an expected "deduction rate" of 20% for taxes and Social Security, and can be overcome if the presumed taxation figures would be incorrect in application to the individual victim. The wage loss benefits would be payable for a maximum of six months from the date of the accident, beginning the first day of wage loss, and there is no waiting period involved. The wage loss benefits are primary coverage, like the medical expenses and again, as with medical expenses, these benefits would be excess coverage over governmental sources. For those individuals not earning wages or such income at the time of the accident, the "wage loss" portion of the Personal Accident Benefit of the Dual Protection Policy would provide for payment of 80% of the "actual dollars spent" in replacing the service normally rendered by the victim, with a maximum of $12 per day.

A "survivor's benefit" is for the benefit of a surviving dependent of the victim, and is payable only if there is a dependent. The Personal Accident Benefit survivor's benefit is 80% of the current wages for the extended period of one year, and is subject to a $500 monthly maximum. Again, in the case of no wages or similar income (such as the non-working mother of a child under the age of 18) the benefit would be $12 a day for the one-year period.

Non-Economic Loss

In addition to the automatic first-party insurance coverages in the Dual Protection Policy, there are some slight but important improvements on the existing tort law system. The first of these involves a reasonable limitation upon recovery for pain and suffering in tort. (The Multiple Benefits Plan does not abolish the individual victim's right to sue in tort, providing he has a suitable case.)

This limitation would expressly not be applied in cases where the injuries from the accident resulted in death, disfigurement, dismemberment, a fracture, temporary or permanent, total or partial disability, or impairment of a bodily function for at least seven days. In addition to these specific exceptions, a jury may in any given tort suit determine that the injuries resulting from the accident were such that the limitation of pain and suffering would be unfair, and the limitation will thus not apply in that case.

Advance Payments

In order to encourage advance payments to victims by liability carriers, it is specifically provided that evidence of such payments will be inadmissible as evidence of liability in any subsequent tort suit resulting from the claim. Nor will such payments be construed as a waiver or estoppel against the company.

Collateral Source Rule

The Collateral Source Rule would probably be altered somewhat in actual operation, even though not in form, by the designation of the Personal Accident Benefit of the Dual Protection Policy as primary insurance. Furthermore, tort recoveries under the Multiple Benefits Plan would be reduced to the extent of any payments which were made to the victim under the Personal Accident Benefit. Thus the benefits from the first-party coverage in the automobile insurance policy itself would not be subject to the Collateral Source Rule.

Judicial Reform

A system of judicial process of arbitration of small claims has been instituted in Pennsylvania for some time. Experience with that system indicates that it has worked fairly satisfactorily as a mechanism for the initial adjudication of automobile accident tort litigation in that jurisdiction where court congestion has resulted in excessive delay in the normal trying of such cases. Such a mechanism may be required in such jurisdictions where court calendar congestion is a serious problem. For that reason the Judicial Reform Proposal has been included in the Multiple Benefits Plan.

Competitive Rating

Another important part of the Multiple Benefits Plan is the provision for competition in automobile insurance rating. Under the proposed "Open Competition Rating Plan" legislation, insurance companies will be free to enter into open price competition with one another in the marketing of insurance policies.

Solvency Assurance

The Multiple Benefits Plan also includes protection for insureds and the industry against possible insolvencies of companies writing this coverage. All insurance companies doing business under the plan will be required to participate in the Automobile Insurance Industry Solvency Assurance Plan, a contractual Plan whereby the obligations of any company becoming insolvent would be assumed (on a proportionate basis) by the other members of the industry.

Market Availability

The Multiple Benefits Plan includes a revised and expanded concept improving upon the assigned risk plans now in operation, in order to alleviate the limited but politically explosive market availability problem which now exists. The Expanded Automobile Insurance Availability Plan is designed so that through its operation even high-risk individuals will be able to obtain higher limits of liability and additional coverages, including, of course, the automatic Personal Accident Benefit of the Dual Protection Policy.

Omnibus Protection

Individuals who are not covered by insurance under the Multiple Benefits Plan will still be provided with insurance benefits to the extent that the gap in coverage is the result of the negligence of another party. The omnibus clause of the Dual Protection Policy extends to automobile accident victims from non-car-owning households (who are those not a part of the Dual Protection Policy market, so that the coverage is not available to them) the Personal Accident Benefit coverages of the Dual Protection Policy applicable to the vehicle involved in the injury.

Assigned Liability Claims

Other individuals may have valid tort claims as the result of injuries caused by the negligence of another, only to find that the claim is unenforceable because the negligent party is uninsured and judgment-proof. Such victims will be able to proceed with their claim under the Multiple Benefits Plan under the Assigned Liability Claims Plan. The claim, under the operation of this plan, will be assigned to a liability insurer (the distribution of such claims being determined proportionately according to business written) for handling. The company will investigate the claim, settle it appropriately, and recover any outlay and expense via subrogation against the tort-feasor.

Public Information and Education

The beneficial effects of deterrence (of negligent driving) and proper allocation of costs (of motoring as a social and economic activity) which flow from the tort law can be maintained only when the public is aware of the goals and method of operation of the system and the effect upon the insurance rates applicable to individuals. The Multiple Benefits Plan thus incorporates legislation establishing the Public Information and Education Model, a program to be administered jointly by the offices of the Insurance Commissioner and the Public Safety Commissioner of the enacting jurisdiction.

Accident Prevention Program

Also established is a program of automobile accident research and prevention, the Automobile Accident prevention Model, to be administered by the same offices The purpose of that program will be investigation into the actual causes of automobile accidents and the implementation of requisite corrective measures.

Classification Rating

It has been previously discussed that classification rating of liability insurance is vital to a system which will continue to support the public desire that costs of automobile accidents be apportioned on a morally acceptable basis. Those individuals who represent the greatest risk must be charged a higher premium, and those individuals representing a lesser risk must be charged lesser premiums. Therefore the Multiple Benefits Plan legislation establishes the "Classification Rating Plan" to achieve this goal.

Allocation of costs as described above is clearly rational as well as morally acceptable. Those individuals contributing proportionately more greatly to the loss pay proportionately higher premiums. Rational allocation of the costs of first-party insurance is much the same. Under first-party insurance, those individuals who create the greatest risk, again, should be rated higher. To the extent to which individuals are negligent drivers, are are likely to be involved in accidents, they do present a proprotionately greater risk, and so to this extent classification rating for first-party insurance in automobile policies would coincide with similar rating under liability insurance. However, individuals who because of their own personal characteristics are likely to present greater claims under first-party insurance ultimately need to be rated higher in order to promote rational allocation of costs, regardless of whether they contribute to a proportionately greater degree to the likelihood of accidents occurring.

The Bases of the Plan

The Multiple Benefits Plan provides, overall, for the maximum compensation of automobile insurance victims. Maximum compensation, of course, is an illusive, comparative and subjective term, over-used in the current discussion of automobile insurance. Maximum compensation, in this context, relates to (1) cost of insurance, (2) number of victims who recover, and

(3) generosity of benefits. When this combination of ingredients is considered, the protection afforded under this plan is, all in all, maximized.

As previously indicated, the highest priority in the criteria of this system is the furtherance of the individual's freedom of choice and action. This freedom is to some degree abrogated inasmuch as the Personal Accident Benefits envisioned under the Multiple Benefits Plan are a mandatory part of the automobile insurance policy. That is, an individual who purchases automobile insurance will be required to purchase a package, which will contain both liability coverages and the first-party insurance coverages. Mandatory coverage is necessary in order to allow the insurance industry to obtain sufficient initial experience to make this plan actuarially sound, to provide more coverage for less cost (e.g. as does the homeowners package plan), and to provide a public education and information function.

It is the intent of the proposed system that small claims be settled primarily by payment under the Personal Accident Benefit. To the extent to which this is the goal which is envisioned, the upper limits on payments under these coverages are rational. It is also envisioned that those individuals who have very large claims will be able to recover their initial out-of-pocket losses and medical expenses.

It is envisioned that individuals who have a valid tort claim will receive primary payment from the liability carrier. Inasmuch as the liability carrier would be subject to subrogation from the first-party insurance payer, the liability carrier should have a direct financial interest in the degree to which the payments made are limited to reasonable and necessary medical expenses and other losses. Clearly the easiest method for the liability carrier to assume control over these expenses is to come into the case itself, making the payments to the victims in advance of the final determination of the claim, and thereby maintaining complete control over the case. The current tendency of liability insurers to fail in this obligation will not continue because, to the extent to which they do not make the payment, the direct insurer will make these payments and will later subrogate against the liability insurer; therefore the insurer has nothing to gain by not paying. There will be no pressure upon the victim to execute a quick compromise agreement, because his expenses, should they be withheld by the liability insurer, will be paid by his first-party coverage. Secondly, advance payments made by the liability carrier will not be admissible in a court of law in a future determination of negligence. Thus, liability insurers need not fear this particular result of making advance payments to the victims.

Subrogation, a characteristic of the present insurance system, is retained under the Multiple Benefits Plan, and functions to shift the loss from the first-party insurance carrier back to either the negligent driver or his liability insurer. Subrogation among the various companies in the insurance industry can and should be achieved with no great expense, friction, or difficulty. To the extent that the liability insurer fails to step quickly into the picture, so that payments are in fact made by the first-party insurance carrier, subrogation between the companies may be complicated if the first-party insurance carrier and the liability carrier have somewhat different claim settlement practices. However, the policyholder will not suffer. He will receive his compensation first, after which the insurance companies can settle their differences by agreement or arbitration.

Basically, the Multiple Benefits Plan provides all victims of automobile accidents an opportunity to recover their basic out-of-pocket losses. The first-party insurance coverage is automatic in every automobile insurance policy, and protection is extended to the named insured in the policy, passengers in the car, and even to uninsured pedestrians (those individuals without access to insurance as a non-automobile owner) whose injuries result from the insured's automobile.

First-party insurance protection for this broad class of automobile insurance victims is designed to compensate them, regardless of negligence or responsibility for the accident, for their initial losses and out-of-pocket expenses. Under such a system, all small claims would be fully compensated, and the immediate needs of the victims who have sustained much larger losses are similarly paid.

The inflated value of nuisance claims is abolished not only by the limitation on pain and suffering, through the elimination of the possibility of padding such small claims through the addition of unreasonable general damages, but also because there will be less need for such padding as a result of the fact that these claims will be paid in full, except for general damages, under first-party insurance coverages. At the same time, individuals with very large losses will be able to resist the temptation to compromise their claims, because their immediate out-of-pocket losses will be covered.

Under the Multiple Benefits Plan, the additional coverages under the first-party insurance provisions of the contract are provided without interfering with the present system's morally appropriate allocation of costs. That is, the tort law system remains effective, and individuals whose negligent driving results in automobile accidents will be held ultimately responsible for the costs resulting from those accidents. Even if individuals are able to escape this burden by obtaining liability insurance, the cost of the system will be proportionately placed upon them through the classification rating system of that liability insurance. Therefore, the morally appropriate allocation of cost is continued.

Those individuals injured on the highway as a result of their own negligence, or as a result of negligence of other parties which cannot be proven, or as a result of accidents which do not result from any negligent driving, will be compensated under the Personal Accident Benefit. The allocation of costs under this system will be morally appropriate, inasmuch as it will be spread amongst the entire motoring public through classification rating. This rating will further assure that the allocation is also rational, because those individuals with the greatest propensity to have claims will be those who bear a proportionately greater percentage of the costs.

The only individuals not provided for under the above system are those individuals who purposely choose to obtain no automobile insurance at all, thereby becoming self-insureds, and who are injured in accidents resulting from their own fault (or at least accidents in which no fault of others is provable). The individual's right and ability to engage in this behavior, at least in regard to insurance protection for his own injuries, is assured as a high priority in America. To the extent, therefore, that individuals use this freedom in an irresponsible manner, and refuse to provide for their needs, and to the combined extent that society takes upon itself voluntarily the duty of compensating these people despite their own voluntary refusal to take care of their own needs, these individuals represent not an automobile accident problem, but a social problem. Such a situation must be cured through education so that these people's value system will be such as to enable them to better function in our complex modern society. At the same time, these individuals will be compensated from general revenue funds, so that the cost of compensating them will be allocated in a morally appropriate manner, equally among the entire society which spawned them and which now takes upon itself the duty of meeting the needs for which they voluntarily refuse to provide.

To the extent to which the deterrent impact of the tort law system operates to discourage negligent and reckless driving, the continuation of that system assures the continued operation of this principle. Indeed, the classification rating under the Multiple Benefits Plan will extend the deterrent effect of the present system, because an individual who drives recklessly, and who is likely to be involved in an accident, will be ultimately penalized not only by high liability insurance rates, but also by high first-party insurance rates, inasmuch as he is not only very likely to cause injuries to another party for which he will be liable, but also to suffer injuries of his own as a result of his negligent conduct. It has been previously pointed out that the primary deterrent effect of the present system, or of any automobile law and insurance system, involves not the dramatic, but improbably, loss which might be expected from being sued for liability, or the even more dramatic, but equally improbable, possibility of suffering grievous injuries in an accident, but rather from a relatively certain penalty imposed by the application of higher insurance rates. This cutting edge of the deterrent principle under the system is improved in effect under the Multiple Benefits Plan.

The Multiple Benefits Plan is designed to be operated by private insurers within the American economy. As such, it will utilize the resources of present insurance companies, present teams of home office personnel, agents, adjusters, and other employees, and who will provide for greater growth of the industry within the system. Designed to meet the problems of our present society, the system demonstrates the way in which private enterprise acts to spur businesses therein to create a better product in order to serve the public.

Through the use of open competition in rating, the Multiple

Benefits Plan assures that all possibilities of income will be taken into consideration by insurance companies. As a result, all competing companies will be encouraged to operate with maximum efficiency, to achieve the greatest amount of income not only as a result of underwriting practices, but also as a result of other business activities, so as to lower the cost of the product available to the public. Other areas of business in the American free enterprise system have shown that cost competition will nearly always result in a better product at a lower cost.

A spin-off of the same reform is that more individuals will be able to receive insurance at lower rates. To the extent to which open competition will allow the industry members to set rates rationally, the classification rating system can be revised, and expanded where indicated, so that individuals can be rated according to their personal driving characteristics more nearly than under the present system with its broad classifications. Even if the lowest insurance rates are not lowered as a result of the system, the system would result in more people being able to get insurance at a lower rate than they now could get it. The problem with the present system is not so much that those individuals who are paying the lowest insurance rate are paying too much, but that those individuals who are paying the higher insurance rates feel that they are paying too much. Under the Multiple Benefits Plan, those individuals would be able to shop for insurance rates upon their own individual characteristics, and the cost of insurance to them would be based upon their own contribution to the risk of loss. In some cases this would result in a lowering of premiums. In other cases, it would result in higher premiums, which would result in a more realistic appraisal by these members of the public of the cost of motoring as they do it.

The Multiple Benefits Plan meets the existing needs of our insurance system through the application of gradual progressive reform. The elements of the Multiple Benefits Plan which represent a change, or progress, from the present system as a whole will continue to function, with changes as indicated by the particular reforms of the Multiple Benefits Plan. The result of such a plan is that these particular reforms can be weighed and evaluated in the future, permitting periodic adjustments as needed. It is unlikely that the behavior of individuals will become harmfully aberrational in anyway as the result of this change of the system, because the change in the system is applied deftly. Unlike massive changes in the entire automobile insurance law system, whereby the behavior of individuals would likely be greatly influenced by the change in the systems, with highly unpredictable results, the Multiple Benefits Plan allows us to continue to solve our problems on the basis of old and familiar principles, while the problems are attacked individually and specifically. This gradual progressive reform does not block further progress upon evaluation of the changes, but to the contrary, allows progressive change to be made in a rational rather than a highly speculative manner.

The Multiple Benefits Plan will operate within the parameters of the American free enterprise system, and it will provide opportunities for extension in growth of the American insurance industry, serving the public under the regulation of the appropriate governmental bodies. As a result, the insurance industry will continue to function in the economy in much the same fashion as it has functioned in the past, even though its activities will be undertaken in a more socially satisfactory manner. The effects of the change upon any individual group in our society will be slight, so that the members of those groups will be able to so adjust their lives as to continue to function in a worthwhile manner under the new system.

The Multiple Benefits Plan is expressly designed to encourage improvement in the design of automoibles and highways. To the extent that the application of this system with classification rating techniques pushes a proportionately greater allocation of the costs upon those drivers who drive cars which tend to be unsafe and cause accidents, the use of such vehicles will be discouraged. At the same time, to the degree to which the same classification system is applied to the first-party insurance coverages results in higher proportionate rates to those people who drive automobiles in which they are likely to suffer greater injuries, the use of those vehicles will be discouraged. In both cases, the allocation of costs under the Multiple Benefits Plan places a high premium upon safe design of motor vehicles, both motor vehicles which are safe to drive, and motor vehicles which are safe to travel in. The latter, of course, is a part of the former, but also has independent ramifications.

Even though the Multiple Benefits Plan provides for allocation of costs on a rational and morally appropriate basis, the underlying base of the rate system must continue to be a function of the degree to which the slaughter on the highways is continued. The Multiple Benefits Plan includes a comprehensive system of education of the public, so that insureds will be aware that their insurance rates are a function of their own driving habits, automobiles that they drive, and the highways upon which they drive. The effect of the system encourages these individuals to improve their driving habits, and be continually aware of the safety of their vehicles, and the safety of the highways upon which they travel. Only an automobile insurance system which provides for classification rating both on the liability insurance and the first-party insurance levels, and which incorporates an allocation of cost based upon negligence and subrogation, can have this effect upon the behavior of insureds, and therefore, through them, upon other segments of society.

Chapter Six

MODEL LEGISLATION

Following is proposed model legislation designed to implement the proposals outlined in the preceding chapter. Only through analysis of the precise language in the model legislation can a technical understanding of the proposal be achieved. The following chapters will then provide some insight into the operation and interrelationship of the various parts of the proposal.

Division I

Section 1. Definitions. For the purposes of this Division, the following terms shall be defined as follows:

1. Bodily Injury. Bodily injury is any bodily injury, sickness, or disease, including death therefrom, arising out of the ownership, maintenance, or use of a motor vehicle as defined herein.

2. Injured Party. An injured party is any party suffering bodily injury, as defined herein.

3. Motor Vehicle. A motor vehicle is any vehicle, including a trailer, used upon the streets, avenues, roads, or highways of this State, or designed to be so used, and which is drawn or propelled by other than muscular power.

4. Commissioner. The Commissioner of Insurance of this State.

5. Policy of Motor Vehicle Liability. Any contract of insurance against loss resulting from liability imposed by law for bodily injury, as defined herein, arising from the ownership, maintenance, or use of a motor vehicle, as defined herein, registered or principally garaged in this state.

Section 2. Personal Accident Coverage. Except as provided in Sub-section 5 herein, no policy of motor vehicle liability insurance shall be delivered, issued for delivery, or continued in force in this State on or after the effective date of this Act unless coverage is provided therein or supplemental thereto affording at least the following minimum benefits:

1. <u>Hospital and Medical Benefits</u>. Payment of all reasonably necessary expenses arising from any motor vehicle accident and incurred within one year from the date thereof for hospital, medical, surgical, dental, optical, radiological, and extended-care services, including but not limited to, prosthetic devices, ambulance services, professional nursing service or care, anesthesiology, and funeral services, up to an aggregate of two thousand dollars per person, provided that reasonable funeral services shall not account for more than one thousand dollars per funeral of that total. Hospital room, or extended-care, and board benefits may be limited to the regular daily semi-private room rates customarily charged by the institution in which the recipient of said benefits is confined.

2. <u>Wage Loss Benefits</u>. In the case of an income producer, payment of benefits equivalent to that person's after-tax loss of income for six months due to the accident, subject to a maximum of $750.00 per month (from the date of the accident). After-tax income shall be presumed to be 80% of that person's gross income at the time of the accident, but this presumption may be rebutted in favor or a higher percentage. Such benefits shall be payable for a maximum of six months, and shall be payable to the injured party periodically, without waiting period, in accordance with Section 4 of this Act. In the case of an injured party not producing income, the benefit shall consist of 80% of the reasonably incurred expense of the substitute help retained to perform services normally performed by that injured party. In this case benefits shall be available on the first day of the loss and for one year thereafter; however, benefits shall be limited to a maximum of twelve dollars per day for a maximum period of six months.

3. <u>Survivor's Benefits</u>. In the event of a death as a result of a motor vehicle accident and if and only if such death occurs within a one year period subsequent to the accident, a Survivor's Benefit shall be payable to the surviving dependent or dependents of the deceased injured party if and only if such surviving dependent or dependents exist. The Surivior's Benefit shall be equivalent to 80% of the gross income of the deceased at the time of the accident, extended for a period of one year, subject to a maximum of $500.00 per month. In the event the deceased produced no income at the time of the accident, the Survivor's Bene-

fit to the dependent or dependents shall be in the amount of twelve dollars per day for the one-year period.

4. Applicability of Benefits. The benefits prescribed in this Section shall be payable as follows:

a. If an injured party owns a valid policy of motor vehicle liability insurance, the insurer selling that policy of motor vehicle liability insurance shall be liable to said injured party, or in the case of the Survivor's Benefit, to the surviving dependent or dependents thereof, for such benefits, provided that if said injured party owns or owned at the time of death, two or more such policies of motor vehicle liability insurance, the insurers selling said policies shall share in said liability on a pro rata basis; or

b. If said injured party is or was at the time of death a member of a household owning or leasing one or more motor vehicles, and any other member or members of said household owns or own a valid policy of motor vehicle liability insurance, the insurer selling that policy of motor vehicle liability insurance shall be liable to said injured party, or in the case of the Survivor's Benefit, to the surviving dependent or dependents thereof, for such benefits, provided that if two or more such policies of motor vehicle liability insurance are owned by such member or members of said household, the insurers selling those policies of motor vehicle liability insurance shall share in said liability on a pro rata basis; or

c. If the injured party is not a member of a household owning or leasing one or more motor vehicles, sustains bodily injury as a result of an accident involving any motor vehicle, the driver or owner of which is insured under a valid policy of motor vehicle liability insurance, the insurer selling such policy of motor vehicle liability insurance shall be liable to said injured party, or in the case of the Survivor's Benefit, to the surviving dependent or dependents thereof, for such benefits, provided that if two or more such policies of motor vehicle liability insurance would be liable therefor herein, the liability shall be shared in by the insurers selling such policies on a pro rata basis.

5. Commissioner Has Power to Grant Exception. Should the owner or operator of any motor vehicle not of the private passenger type, or fleet of such motor vehicles, feel unduly prejudiced by the requirements of this Section, he may request a

hearing with the Commissioner, which hearing the Commissioner shall hold within fifteen days. If at said hearing said owner or operator adduces, to the satisfaction of the Commissioner, proof of financial responsibility adequate to provide benefits and re-imbursements of benefits as prescribed in Subsections 1, 2, and 3 of this Section as directed by Subsection 4 of this Section and Section 5 of this Division, the Commissioner shall, and is here-by empowered to, grant an exception to this Section and allow a policy of motor vehicle liability insurance to be issued for de-livery and delivered to said owner or operator, which policy need not contain the provision of said benefits; provided, however, that in the event of an accident involving any motor vehicle so insured, said owner or operator shall be liable as the insurer selling said policy of motor vehicle liability insurance for said benefits as though they were provided under that policy of motor vehicle lia-bility insurance; provided also that such owner and operator as a condition of being granted said exception, shall be deemed to have agreed as an insurer to the agreement contained in Section 5 of this Division.

6. <u>Policyholder has option to Cancel Personal Accident Cov-erage</u>. Except as provided in Sub-section 5 herein, no policy of motor vehicle liability insurance shall be delivered, issued for delivery, or continued in force in this state on or after the effective date of this Act unless it shall contain a standardized form, according to such specifications as shall be designated by the office of the Commissioner of Insurance, the completion of which, in triplicate, requiring some minimal amount of informa-tion concerning the financial status of the policyholder, and sub-mission of which, either in person or by mail, of two copies to the issuing office of the company (one of which shall be forwarded to the Commissioner), shall be required as a condition precedent to the cancellation of the Personal Accident Coverage. Upon re-ceipt of such forms properly completed with all required infor-mation and request for cancellation, the issuing company shall cancel the Personal Accident Coverage portion of the policy, and refund to the policyholder within a reasonable time such return premium as shall be due under the normal procedures for can-cellations at the policyholder's request.

<u>Section 3. Benefits as Primary Insurance</u>. The coverage pre-

scribed by Section 2 of this Division shall be considered primary and not excess insurance, except that the Hospital and Medical Benefits, and the Wage Loss Benefits prescribed in Subsections 1 and 2 of that Section shall be considered excess insurance with respect to proceeds from any workmen's compensation plan, Medicare plan, or similar governmental source, on account of the bodily injury sustained.

Section 4. Payment of Benefits. All payments of benefits prescribed under Section 2 of this Division shall be made periodically as claims therefore arise and as promptly as satisfactory proof thereof is received by the insurance company. The existence of a cause of action, or claim for which relief may be granted, in tort in any person entitled to the receipt of benefits prescribed in Section 2 of this Division shall not obviate the insurer's obligation to promptly pay such benefits; provided that if prior to timely payment by the insurer of such benefits, payment in whole or in part of any person's loss is received by that person from a third person who is or may be liable in tort for such loss, or from the agent or insurer of such third person for or on that person's account, either by way of advance payment or settlement of the potential liability of such third person, the recipient shall disclose such fact and may not collect benefits hereunder to the extent that such benefits would produce a duplication of payment or reimbursement of the same loss.

Section 5. Subrogation. To the extent of the payment of any benefits provided pursuant to Section 2 of this Division, or of any other direct insurance benefits payable in accordance with the provisions of any automobile insurance policy unless otherwise provided in the policy, the insurer making said payment or payments shall be subrogated to the beneficiary's rights of recovery therefore against any person or organization who might be liable to said beneficiary for the losses or expenses compensated by said benefits. Every insurer licensed to write motor vehicle liability insurance in this state shall as a condition to maintaining such license after the effective date of this Act, where its insured is or would be held legally liable for damages so paid, upon demand, reimburse such other insurer to the extent of such payments but not in excess of the amount of damages recoverable for the type of loss covered by such benefits. Every insurer shall pursue and collect all such subrogation claims against any party liable, to the full extent of the law; except that in the case of claims against another insurance company, claims may be dropped when the cost of pursuing the claim would demonstrably exceed the expected gross recovery, and claims may be pursued by any method of administrative annual accounting, or otherwise, if so provided by the Commissioner of Insurance, in accordance with Division of this Act.

Section 6. Limits of Liability. No policy of motor vehicle insurance as defined in Section 1 of this Division shall be delivered or issued for delivery in this state on or after the effective date of this Act unless the limits of liability for bodily injury contained therein are at least adequate to compensate liability for bodily injury damages in the amount of one hundred thousand dollars.

Section 7. Expanded Benefits. The benefits and limits of liability prescribed in Sections 2 and 6 of this division are minimum benefits only, and in no way shall any Section or Subsection of this act be construed or interpreted as to prevent any insurer from making available, at the option of the consumer, expanded or increased benefits and limits of liability.

Section 8. General Repealer. All acts and parts of acts inconsistent with this Act are hereby repealed as of the effective date of this Act.

Section 9. Effective Date. This Act shall become effective at 12:01 A.M. on Jan. 1 of the year following its enactment.

Division 2

Assigned Liability Claims Plan

Sec. 1: For the purposes of this division, unless the context requires otherwise:

(1) "Insurance Company" means a company licensed to sell automobile liability insurance in this state.

(2) "Injured Person" means a person who has sustained bodily injury, sickness or disease, including death resulting therefrom, or injury or destruction to property, including loss of use thereof, which in his opinion is recoverable in tort against a party responsible for causing said loss.

(3) "Assigned Claim" is an application for recovery for a loss sustained by an injured person or insurance company that is presented to the Insurance Department.

(4) "Assigned Claims Plan" means a program for the assignment of liability claims administered by the Insurance Department.

(5) "Administrator" is the person appointed by the Insurance Commissioner to administer the assigned claims program.

Sec. 2 The Commissioner of Insurance shall hereby establish the Assigned Claims Plan in accordance with the provisions of this act. This Plan shall be supervised and directed as determined by the Commissioner, and, with the approval of the Commissioner, rules shall be adopted to assist the accomplishment of the intent and purposes of this act. The Commissioner may delegate administrative duties, in his discretion.

Sec. 3 Any injured person, who, as the result of the operation of an uninsured motor vehicle, sustains a loss which, in his opinion, would be otherwise an uncollectible claim may make application for assignment claim, to the Assigned Claims Plan. The administrator shall forthwith, without regard to the merits of the claim, assign the claim to one of the insurance companies in this state. The administrator shall fairly and equitably assign claims to insurance companies in proportion to the volume of automobile liability insurance premiums the companies are writing in this State. A company must accept assignment of a claim in order to continue to sell automobile insurance in this State. If a company feels the assignment was not made in a fair and equitable manner, it may appeal the decision of the administrator to the Insurance Commissioner who shall review the decision. The decision of the Commissioner to uphold or revoke the assignment is final.

Sec. 4 The insurance company, upon receiving the assigned

claim, shall investigate the validity of the claim in the same manner as it would investigate any other claim made against it under the provisions of the automobile liability insurance policy approved for sale in this State. The company may settle or deny the claim according to its usual standards. Any settlement made shall be up to but not to exceed the current liability limits established by the financial responsibility laws of this State. As a condition of accepting settlement from an insurance company under the provisions of this division, the injured person or company shall assign all rights of subrogation to the insurance company making the settlement.

Sec. 5 An insurance company that has settled an assigned claim under the provisions of the Assigned Claims Plan shall to the maximum extent feasible pursue its subrogation rights against the party responsible for causing said loss. Any recovery from a responsible party received by an insurance company which exceeds the settlement made with the injured person shall be refunded to the injured person. Upon completion of its pursuit of its subrogation rights, or each year, which ever comes first, the insurance company shall file a full report of the companies actions on said claim on forms provided for that purpose by the Administrator.

Division 3

Advance Payments

Sec. 1 In any action in which the defendant, his insurer or any other person has made an advance payment to or on behalf of any claimant prior to trial, any evidence of or concerning said advance payment shall not be admissible in evidence (or as an admission against liability) in any action brought by the claimant, his survivors or personal representative, to recover damages for personal injuries or for the wrongful death of another, or for property damage or destruction.

Sec. 2 In the event, however, that such action results in a verdict in favor of the claimant (in excess of payments) the defendant shall be allowed to introduce evidence of such payments af-

81

ter the verdict has been rendered and the court shall then reduce the amount awarded to the claimant by the amount of payments made prior to trial.

Sec. 3 No such payment made pursuant to the provision of this section by an insurer on behalf of an insured shall be construed to be in lieu of or in addition to the limits of liability of the insurer under any existing policy of insurance, but such sums paid in advance shall be deemed to have been made pursuant to the limits of the policy and shall be credited to the insurer's obligation to the insured arising from such policy and shall be deducted therefrom.

Sec. 4 For the purpose of subsection 1 above, the word "advance payment" shall be construed to include, but not limited to the following: any partial payment, loan or settlement made by any person, corporation or insurer thereof, to another which is predicated upon possible tort liability or under the contractual obligations of the insurer to the injured party or on his behalf, including but not limited to medical, surgical, hospital, rehabilitation services, facilities or equipment, loss of earnings, out-of-pocket expenses, death claims, loans, bodily injury or property damage, loss or destruction.

Sec. 5 This statute shall be applicable to any action commenced in this state, regardless of the situs of the accident, location of the property or residence of the parties.

Sec. 6 The making of an advance payment shall not interrupt the running of the Statute of Limitations, provided that any person, including any insurer, who makes such advance payment, shall at the time of the first payment, notify the recipient thereof in writing of the date the applicable statute will expire and that such payments do not toll same.

Sec. 7 Any advance payment made under this section shall be considered non-refundable, and in the event the legal liability of the person or insurer advancing said payment is not established, the claimant shall not be required to return said payment.

Division 4

Contributory Negligence

Sec. 1 Contributory negligence shall not bar recovery in an action by any person or his legal representative to recover damages for negligence resulting in death or in injury to person or property, if such negligence was not as great as the negligence of the person against whom recovery is sought, but any damages allowed shall be diminished in the proportion to the amount of negligence attributable to the person recovering.

Division 5

Compulsory Arbitration Provision

Sec. 1 The Insurance Commissioner of this State is hereby empowered to make and enforce rules requiring the settlement of subrogation claims or of all claims under $1000.00 by arbitration, or of subrogation claims by such other administrative method as shall be feasible, when in his opinion such arbitration or other method of settlement becomes necessary. Such rules shall apply only in those areas and during those periods designated by the Commissioner.

Sec. 2 In the event this should take place, the Commissioner shall provide rules providing for the appeal of any arbitration decision to a Court of original jurisdiction in this State where the action shall be heard de novo, that any payment of costs required by rule in order to appeal said decision not exceed in the case of claims other than subrogation claims, fifty (50) dollars.

Division 6

Open Competition Rating

Sec. 1 Rates for automobile insurance shall not be excessive, inadequate, or unfairly discriminatory. Insurance companies are authorized to establish and operate qualified rating organizations provided that specific rating services of such rating or-

83

ganizations be generally available to all admitted insurers. The Commissioner of insurance shall have no power to fix or determine a rate level by classification or otherwise.

Sec. 2 Insurance companies may act in concert with each other and with others with respect to any matters pertaining to the making of rates or rating systems, underwriting rules, surveys, inspections, investigations, the furnishing of loss statistics, or carrying on of research. The companies may use the rates of rating systems of a rating organization but shall not agree with each other or the rating organization to adhere thereto.

<u>Division 7</u>

<u>Solvency Assurance</u>

An Act relating to the solvency of insurance companies.

Sec. 1 Definitions: For the purposes of this Act, unless the context requires otherwise:
1. "Automobile Insurance Solvency Board" means a board established by the automobile insurance companies, which shall prevent financial loss to policy holders due to the insolvency of one or more insurance companies.
2. "Insurance companies" means any insurance company, foreign or domestic, that is admitted to market automobile insurance in this state.
3. "Policyholders" means any person who has an automobile insurance policy that was delivered or issued for delivery in this State.
4. "Solvency Assurance Fund" means the monies that may be raised by the assessment of insurance companies by the Solvency Assurance Board.
5. "Contribution" means the amount of assessment that may be required of an individual insurance company for the Solvency Insurance Fund.

Sec. 2 In accordance with rules and regulations of the Insurance Department, the Automobile Insurance companies shall establish an "Automobile Insurance Solvency Board." The board shall be established for the purpose of preventing or protecting the insurance buying public from financial loss resulting from the insolvency of automobile insurance companies.

Sec. 3 In the event an insurance company doing business in this State is declared insolvent according to laws of this State the Automobile Insurance Solvency Board shall as soon as possible determine the estimated total dollar loss to the policy holder of this State due to said insolvency. Upon a determination of the estimated loss, the Board would require a contribution to the Solvency Assurance Fund within 30 days from each insurance company writing automobile insurance in this State in proportion to the dollar volume of automobile insurance premiums written in this State. No contribution however, in any one year, may exceed one (1) per cent of a company's total auto insurance premiums in this State, and to the extent the contribution of a company may be inadequate because of this limitation, the unpaid balance of said company's share shall be reassessed in a like manner amongst the remaining companies.

Sec. 4 The solvency Assurance Fund, once created, shall be used by the Automobile Insurance Solvency Board to meet the obligation of the insolvent company created by their automobile insurance policies only. In the event the Board pays a claimant for which the insolvent company is liable, the company shall be liable to the Board to the extent of such payment and in the same manner and degree the company would have been liable to the claimant.

Sec. 5 If the estimated contributions fall short of satisfying the accumulated claims of the insolvent company, the Board shall reassess another contribution from the insurance companies in the same manner as it assessed the original contributions. If, however, the estimated amount in the solvency assurance fund exceeded that necessary to pay the claims, the Board may refund the surplus to the companies or hold and invest the funds, whichever it deems more practical. The manner and time for determining claimants to the Solvency Assurance Form shall be determined by the Insurance Commissioner.

Sec. 6 Each insurance company shall, at its own expense, be audited annually by a certified public accounting agency, and the results of such audit shall be immediately be made available to the Automobile Insurance Solvency Board. The Board shall report the results of the audit to the Insurance Commissioner. In the event the financial stability of an insurance company is not in accord with generally accepted criteria for the industry, any and all reports shall be immediately made available to the Commissioner.

Sec. 7 The Department of Insurance is hereby empowered to make rules to carry out the intent and purpose of this act.

Division 8

Public Information and Education

Sec. 1 The Insurance Commissioner, in conjunction with the Department of Public Safety, shall establish a program to educate and inform the general public of the basic principles of the automobile insurance system, and of the responsibilities of policyholders and insurers under its provisions. In particular, this program shall specifically inform the public of the basis of the rate making of the automobile insurance companies, emphasizing that the motorists deemed to be most likely to cause accidents must pay proportionately higher premiums, and that uninsured motorists are actually self-insured, and fully responsible.

Division 9

Automobile Accident Prevention Model

Sec. 1 The Insurance Commissioner, in conjunction with the Department of Public Safety, shall establish a program to investigate the actual causes of automobile accidents. The program shall be specifically designed to pinpoint the characteristics of motor vehicles, drivers, and highways which contribute to accidents, and other characteristics or practices which so contribute.

Sec. 2 All insurance companies doing business in this state shall, determine the cause of any accident which is the basis of an insurance claim, to the best of their ability as required by the claims process, and shall record the information so obtained. Such information must be forwarded to the Insurance Commissioner at intervals of once per year, as designated by the Commissioner.

Sec. 3 The Insurance Commissioner is empowered to recommend to the legislature, upon the basis of the information gained through the Automobile Accident Prevention Model, appropriate remedial legislation.

Division 10

Severability

If any provision of this Act is declared unconstitutional, or the applicability thereof to any person or circumstance is held invalid the constitutionality of the remainder of the Act and the applicability thereof to other persons and circumstances shall not be afflicted thereby.

Division 11

Noneconomic Loss

An award for general damages or pain and suffering shall be abrogated, except in instances where the accident resulted in death, disfigurement, dismemberment, a fracture, temporary or permanent partial or total disability, or impairment of a body function for at least seven days. In addition to these specific exceptions, a jury may in any given tort suit determine that the injuries resulting from the accident were such that the limitation of pain and suffering would be unfair, and the limitation will not apply in that case.

Classification and Merit Rating

No insurer may deliver, issue for delivery, or continue in force any policy of motor vehicle insurance in this state on or after the effective date of this act unless the policy has been rated, to determine premiums, in a manner so designed that the premium for each coverage shall be higher for insureds who are more likely to cause injury or to be injured resulting thereby in damages. The rating must reflect potential damage possibilities of the individual driver.

COMMENTS BY SECTION

Division 1

Section 1.

1. Bodily injury is defined in Subsection 1 using the definition commonly supplied in most motor vehicle liability and medical payments insurance policies. As this is the type of injury with which this division is concerned, that definition is felt appropriate.

2. Injured party is definite in Subsection 2, in terms relating to the definition of bodily injury in Subsection 1.

3. Motor vehicle, as defined in Subsection 3, is intended to include all automobiles, trucks, buses, motorcycles, etc.; and also includes any type of vehicle when used on the public roads. In addition, this definition includes any vehicle designed to be used on the public roads no matter how it is actually used. Thus an accident involving, for example, two automobiles but occurring in a private driveway is within the scope of this definition.

4. Commissioner is defined in Subsection 4. This definition is self-explanatory.

5. The definition of policy of motor vehicle liability insurance in Subsection 5 is couched in terms similar to the terms of the bodily injury liability section of the standard Family Automobile Policy of insurance. This definition includes all types of automobile bodily injury insurance, and also includes any pol-

icy of insurance designed to protect the insured from liability
due to bodily injury associated with any motor vehicle, as defined in this section.

Section 2.

This section mandatorily attaches the Personal Accident
Coverage to any motor vehicle liability insurance within the jurisdiction of the state, except as provided in Subsection 5, and thus
makes any such insurance policy into the type envisioned by the
Dual Protection Plan.

1. Subsection 1 specifies the minimum benefits provided under the Hospital and Medical portion of the Personal Accident
Coverage plan. These benefits are designed to pay the accident
victim's immediate out-of-pocket costs related to hospitalization
and medical care. The Subsection is worded similarly to the
medical insurance portion of the Family Automobile Policy, but
also specifically includes provisions for extended care benefits.
The specific provision of these extended care benefits is hoped to
encourage both accident victims and incurers to use the less expensive extended care facilities whenever possible, thus saving
money for the insurer, and ultimately, the insured.

2. Subsection 2 prescribes the Wage Loss Benefits provided
for the accident victim during incapacity, setting out the measure
of benefits, and the maximum amount and time period of payment of these benefits.

3. Subsection 3 provides a Survivor's Benefit for the surviving dependent of an accident victim. In this way the dependent
or dependents of the accident need not suffer financially in any
case, assuming the victim was insured: If the victim is injured,
the Wage Loss benefits maintain income of the dependent or dependents during the victim's incapacity, and if the victim is killed
the Survivor's Benefits do the same.

4. Subsection 4 prescribes who shall receive benefits from
whom. If an accident victim owns insurance incorporating the
Personal Accident Coverage, his insurer pays him the benefits.
If the victim is a member of a household in which someone else
owns this type of insurance, the insurer selling that policy pays
his benefits. If the victim is not a member of a household owning or leasing motor vehicles, and is involved in an accident also
involving a motor vehicle insured under a policy containing the

Personal Accident Coverage, the insurer selling that policy pays his benefits. Where two or more policies are involved in any of these three situations, the payment of the benefits is shared <u>pro rata</u>. It will be noticed from the wording of this Subsection that these classes are mutually exclusive: Thus, no victim may recover more than once under the provisions of this Subsection. It will also be noticed that there are only two possible cases which an accident victim will receive no Personal Accident Benefits: Where the victim is a member of a household owning or leasing a motor vehicle, which includes the possibility that he himself owns or leases it, and neither the victim or any member of his household owns a policy of insurance containing the provision of the Personal Accident Compensation benefits; and where the victim, not being a member of a household owning or leasing automobiles (and hence unable to buy insurance containing the provision of the Personal Accident Benefits) is injured in an accident involving only motor vehicles which are uninsured. In either case, if the accident is the fault of another party, the victim is assured recovery under negligence principles, under the assigned claims plan.

5. Subsection 5 contains provisions for the Commissioner of Insurance to grant an exception to the mandatory inclusion of the Personal Accident Benefits in any policy of motor vehicle insurance applied to vehicles not of the private passenger type. This exception may be granted when the Commissioner is convinced of the financial ability of the person seeking the exception to provide the benefits prescribed to whomever his insurer would be required to provide benefits in the case of an accident. Presumably, this financial ability would be demonstrated by sufficient other insurance or independent wealth. As a condition of this exception being granted, the party to whom it is granted assumes the responsibilities his insurer would have for the payment of these benefits, and also agrees to the subrogation agreement which renders him liable for all benefits paid under this plan by anyone to persons injured in a motor vehicle accident for which he is at fault. (Such a person could well consider the ramifications of driving his automobile into a bus filled with fifty or sixty octogenarians living in a home for the aged.) This section is provided primarily for the benefit of large corporate concerns operating transportation facilities, for whom it might be more

efficient to provide for these benefits from a policy of general liability insurance, or out of working capital.

6. This section provides a method of cancellation of the Personal Accident Benefit. The method is sufficiently troublesome and devoid of immediate financial return to assure its nonuse by the average policyholder, so as to induce an almost universal class of Personal Accident Benefit insureds without resort to arbitrary compulsion in the care of those few individuals who for valid and important reasons, as manifested by their compliance with this cumbersome procedure, desire to not be provided this coverage.

Section 3.

This section provides that the insurance provided by the Personal Accident Coverage is primary and not excess coverage. Making this coverage primary coverage makes the cost of motoring directly payable by the motoring public, instead of spreading those costs over the society as a whole.

Section 4.

This section specifies the time and method of payment of the benefits provided by the Personal Accident Coverage insurance, and prevents double recovery by the accident victim. It will be noted that benefits are payable as soon as the insurer receives proof of loss, and that these payments are not to be delayed by the possibility of a tort recovery for the losses to be compensated by the benefits.

It is anticipated, however, that the combination of provisions in the plan will result, in most cases, in payments by the potentially liable liability insurer, who will wish to control the payments rather than be subjected to a subrogation action by the victims insurer.

Section 5.

Section 5 subrogates the insurer paying benefits as provided in the Personal Accident Coverage to the rights of the recipient of those benefits to the extent of the benefits paid. This section also contains an insurer's subrogation agreement in which any insurer retaining its license after the effective date of the act agrees to reimburse anyone paying the benefits provided by the

Personal Accident Coverage as a result of a motor vehicle accident in which that insurer's insured is determined to be at fault. It should be noted that Section 2 of Subsection 5 makes this agreement applicable to those obtaining the Commissioner's grant of exception to the mandatory inclusion of this insurance in all motor vehicle policies.

The insurer's subrogation agreement in section 5 is intended to encourage insurers who feel that their insured is liable in a motor vehicle accident to assume the burden of paying benefits to all victims of that accident, as explained in the preceding comment. In this way the insurer assuming the burden of making the benefit payment would be able to control the method and amount of benefits disbursed, and should its insured be found not at fault in the accident, that insurer would be subrogated by this Section to the extent of the payments made by it, rather than the reverse. During the time prior to determination of fault, therefore, vitally important to the victim, he should find both insurers anxious to pay, rather than the contrary.

Section 6.

All previous sections have dealt with the problems of getting prompt compensation to the motor vehicle accident victim, and then morally allocating the costs of this compensation. Section 6 deals with another part of the motor vehicle accident problem: The catastrophic loss. While it is not contended that establishing minimum limits for motor vehicle bodily injury liability insurance of one hundred thousand dollars, as this Section does, will alleviate entirely the undercompensation of accident victims suffering catastrophic losses, the work done by this Section represents a first step in solving the catastrophic loss problem. The limits could be lowered to $50,000 or $25,000 if required as a matter of political necessity, or, hopefully, raised to provide unlimited coverage where possible.

Through the assigned claims plan all victims injured as the result of the negligence of another would be assured recovered. Those injured to this catastrophic extent through their own negligence would hopefully be cared for, like similar victims of non-motoring catastrophes, through other societal means.

Section 7.

Here it is provided that additional benefits may be made available.

Section 8.

Self-explanatory.

Section 9.

Self-explanatory.

Division 2

This section provides an assigned liability claims plan, under which plan every victim of an automobile accident will have access to an automobile liability insurance policy. Under the assigned claims plan, the insurance company assignee, once the claim is assigned to it, shall handle the claim just as though the defendant in the claim were one of its ordinary automobile liability insureds.

Section 5 provides that the insurance company handling an assigned claim must pursue its subrogation rights against the tort-feasor. Knowledge of this requirement, through the public education program, will hopefully serve to provide an additional inducement to the purchase of automobile liability insurance.

Division 3

The sections of this division are designed to encourage advanced payments on the part of liability insurers, by specifically attacking those difficulties which have lead in the part to insurance company fears regarding such payments. These provisions, in conjunction with others, are part of a package designed to encourage prompt and fair settlements by liability insurers.

Division 4

Self-explanatory.

Division 5

Here the Insurance Commissioner is empowered, if nec-

essary (as, for example, in the case of excessive court congestion in certain metropolitan areas), to provide for the compulsory arbitration of claims. Such arbitration, however, would
only be required in the particular areas and during the particular
periods of time that the necessity existed.

The Insurance Commissioner, in regard to subrogation
claims, could require either arbitration or such other administrative methods as was deemed feasible. Many such methods
are currently in use in the insurance industry, providing a maximum of effective cost allocation with a minimum of administrative distress, and such methods could readily be continued or
expanded under this section.

Division 6

The effect of this section is discussed at length in upcoming
chapters.

Division 7

This section and its effects are discussed at length in upcoming chapters.

Division 8

The most obvious and glaring overwhelming truth to come
out of all of the research into systems of automobile accident
reparations is that members of the public are grieviously unaware of the policy, methodology, or ramifications of this area
of our society. Individual freedom and responsibility, keystones
of this plan, can only remain in effect through the activities of an
educated public. Individual citizens cannot be expected to meet
responsibilities of which they are unaware, or to make rational
choices amongst alternatives which are unclear to them. Rather
than abrogate the principles of individual freedom and responsibility, as so many other proposals have done, this section provides a mechanism whereby members of the public will be educated in order to obtain the maximum benefit from their individual choices.

Division 10

Self-explanatory.

Division 11

This provision is designed to minimize the "nuisance claim" problem by providing a reasonable limitation upon general damages in the smaller claims, without completely abrogating that valuable right. In the interest of equity, "larger" cases are not defined by an arbitrary dollar limit, but rather by the type and consequences of the injury.

Division 12

Self-explanatory. To be discussed in detail in a later chapter.

Chapter Seven

THE "DUAL PROTECTION" AUTOMOBILE
INSURANCE POLICY IN DETAIL

The Personal Accident Benefit (the first-person medical coverages of the Dual Protection Policy) provides for the payment of all reasonable medical, surgical, hospital and related expenses incurred by the victim within one year of the accident. These "reasonable expenses" include a semi-private hospital room and related hospital and doctor's expenses, in accordance with current health insurance plans. Such expenses are subject to a $2,000 maximum amount, but that maximum could be raised or lowered to the extent that the industry, the public, or a legislature felt necessary. Philosophically, there need be no limit, certainly no limit this low, upon the maximum benefits to be paid under this coverage, but there are three factors which serve to support the imposition of a limit. First, the purpose of this coverage is not to substitute for either tort liability of sufficient independent first-party insurance, but rather to compensate all automobile accident victims for their immediate "out-of-pocket" expenses. The $2,000 maximum limit is appropriate for this goal. Second, in order for this coverage to be feasible for all insureds, even high-risk insureds, it is necessary that the limits of coverage not be excessive, at least during the initial interim while loss experience is being obtained. Third, it is important that the liability limits remain sufficiently higher than the first-party limits that the liability carrier will be induced to step into. The Personal Accident Benefit limits, then, are a function of the liability limits. Both may be too low in the $2,000-$10,000 range, but the first-party limits may be raised only when a greater raise in the liability limits is also feasible. In the event of death, any unused medical coverage may be applied to funeral expense, with an upper limit for the latter of $1,000.

The medical coverage of the Dual Protection Policy is designated "primary insurance" for automobile accidents. It would be anticipated that, upon acceptance of this provision of the Dual Protection Policy, health and accident insurers, group insurers, and other carriers might rapidly designate their policies as "excess insurance" over the Personal Accident Benefit protection. Such a designation would enable premiums to be reduced for those carriers, and therefore make those policies more easily and successfully marketable. Motorists insured under the Dual Protection Policy normally would be subject to lower rates for their other first-party medical coverages than other consumers because of the effect of the Personal Accident Benefit in lowering the probability that excess coverage would be required to pay benefits in the event of loss. Other such policies at the same time, might require a higher premium and might not be designated excess over the Personal Accident Benefit. Here again, then, the consumer's wide range of choice is maximized.

The designation of the medical coverages in the Dual Protection Policy as "primary" is supportable not only on the above practical basis, but is also philosophically sound. To the extent to which injuries result from automobile accidents, their payment under the Personal Accident Benefit as primary coverage will tend to insure that the cost of these accidents, is reflected in the cost of automobile insurance, therefore providing a more realistic measure of the cost of motoring in our society.

The Personal Accident Benefit provisions for the payment of lost wages provides for compensation in lieu of current wages up to a maximum of $750 per month. This benefit is payable for six months following the accident, becoming effective on the first day of wage loss. (Social Security disability benefits become effective six months after the accident.) The problems of defining wages or income, and of evaluating the amount of wages, will be solved in accordance with current disability insurance principles.

Payment is not made to the victim for the full current wages, even up to the maximum of $750 per month, but rather the wages are reduced by 20%, so that the victim receives 80% of his current wages. This reduction represents an explicit recognition of the fact that the insurance benefits are non-taxable whereas ordinary wages or other income received is taxable. The 80% limitation is based upon the assumption that the victim would pay 15% of his before-tax wages in the form of federal taxes, and an additional 5% in the form of Social Security and related deductions, and state taxes, so that his after-tax income (this after-tax income being that which is being replaced by the wage loss benefits) would be only 80% of his before-tax income. The accident reparation, of course, will be tax free. The intent of the benefit is to compensate the victim in full (up to the maximum "per month" limitation) for his actual, after-tax, income. The 80% limitation, therefore, is simply a mechanical presumption designed to facilitate, without controversy, the payment of the wages. To the extent to which an individual victim can demonstrate that his actual after-tax income was a larger percentage (than 80%) of his before-tax income, he will receive the larger percentage under his wage loss benefit.

As is medical expense, the wage loss benefit is designated "primary" insurance; and once again, the wage loss benefit is excess insurance over governmental sources. The rationale for this characteristic, both as a practical and as a philosophical matter, is identical with that for the medical insurance benefits. The rationale is even stronger as applied to loss of income; however, because of the inducement to malinger which exists as long as a disabled victim might be enabled to purchase (or collect from) insurance in such combination that his income from the payments in the event of disability would be in excess of his income upon returning to activity, double recovery should not be allowed to occur in the absence of appropriate consideration, express provisions and collection of premiums (either directly, or indirectly as in the case of the inclusion of a "wage continuation play" as a "fringe benefit" of an employment contract.)

Wage loss benefits should be adaptable to the situation in which individuals suffer injury, and incur economic loss from their inactivity, even though they do not generally earn wages. The classic example of this situation is the housewife, whose activities around the home (cooking, cleaning, babysitting, chauffering, etc.) are valuable, and must be supplied in many cases by paid help in her absence, but are not usually compensated on a salary basis. At the same time, payment of benefits to such individuals based on potential income, or assumed income, or quantum meruit, is an extremely dangerous proposition, inasmuch as there are no real objective standards by which the value of their activity can be measured, and the claims for payment may be therefore subject to the dangers of both capriciousness and fraud. To the extent to which such damages are recoverable in tort there is less of a problem, inasmuch as the burden is in tort cases placed upon the victim to demonstrate, with sufficient proof to meet the legal standards, that the losses in fact exist, and that the amount claimed is reasonable and in accordance with the facts. This standard of proof, however, cannot be realistically employed in a first-party insurance situation because the cooperative relationship between an insured and his insurer is such that the evidence applicable in an adversary situation becomes unreasonable. Therefore some other method of determining the degree of compensation of these individuals must be determined.

Bearing in mind that the purpose of the direct insurance coverages under the Dual Protection Policy is not to provide full individually-tailored compensation for each victim, but rather to compensate these victims for their immediate "out-of-pocket" losses, the losses resulting from injuries to persons who do not receive regular wages or income can fairly easily be determined in a manner commensurate with that goal. To the extent to which the services of the victim are actually replaced, for pay, by a third party who is in the business of performing such services for hire, the Personal Accident Benefit provides for compensation of the victim for the actual expense of replacing the lost services. Here, then, the "wage loss" portion of the Personal Accident Benefit of the Dual Protection Policy would provide for payment of 80% of the actual dollars spent. Here the 80% limitation is the same as under the wage replacement, but for different reasons. Rehabilitation of victims can be hastened by the provision of reasonable incentives to return to normal activity as soon as feasible, and this 80% limitation provides such incentive. The 20% co-insurance is designed to provide the incentive while still removing the traumatic characteristics of the total expense insurred. As under wage loss coverage, this coverage is effective the first day of loss, and extends for one year thereafter.

Also important are the removal of a large part of the inducement to fraud and the discouraging of malingering. All of the above should further operate to prevent abuse of this feature of the Personal Accident Benefit and therefore to reduce the premiums attributable to this coverage. These payments are subject to a maximum of $12 per day, or $4,380 per year. The losses are payable for a period of one year from the date of the accident.

Just as there are victims who do not qualify for wage loss benefits under the Personal Accident Benefit, and who are therefore provided with the alternate benefits described above, there are those individuals who will suffer as a result of a loss of income but who do not qualify for the wage loss benefits because they are _indirect_ victims. Such victims are the dependents who suffer from the loss of the income of a breadwinner who has died as a result of injuries in an automobile accidnet. The Dual Protection Policy provides a "survivors" benefit for such individuals. This part of the Personal Accident Benefit is payable only if an automobile accident victim dies as a result of his injuries within one year of the accident, and is payable only if there is a dependent. The amount of the benefit is $6,000. This amount, like the limits applicable to the other coverages, will be subject to change as the cost or standard of living changes, or as liability limits increase.

Chapter Eight

ADDITIONAL LEGISLATION INCLUDED

Non-Economic Loss

The tort law revision in the Multiple Benefits Plan which limits recovery for pain and suffering represents one solution to the complex problem presented by the malapportionment of benefits. Under the present system, because of the possibility of an inflated pain and suffering claim resulting from an accident of relatively little severity, and the possibility that such claims might result in excessive verdicts if taken to court (even though the probability is slight), such claims have a certain nuisance value over and above that value which might ordinarily be ascribed to the claim. Conversely, those very severe claims in which the provable direct losses are very large, are of such financial impact that the individual victim seldom recovers a high percentage of his losses. As a result of these contrary situations, very small claims tend to be compensated very generously, while very large claims tend to be compensated less generously. The Multiple Benefits Plan's limitation upon recovery for pain and suffering is directly addressed to this malapportionment of benefits.

To the extent to which a small claim is not based upon injuries which resulted in death, disfigurement, dismemberment, a fracture, temporary or permanent total or partial disability, or impairment of a body function for at least seven days, the claim is not likely to present a high valid claim for pain and suffering, or general damages.

The examination of pain and suffering are not actually awards given in compensation for pain as such, but rather as "general damages" awarded for the indignities suffered by the victim, and the disruption of his life style throughout his future, usually not measurable by provable specific damages. Realistically, losses of this nature are not likely to occur in cases where the claim is small or is not a result of death, disfigurement, dismemberment, a fracture, temporary or permanent total or partial disability, or impairment of a body function for at least seven days.

The catastrophic loss which occurs is catastrophic because the injuries have resulted in death, disfigurement, dismemberment, a fracture, temporary or permanent total or partial disability, or impairment of a body function for at least seven days. Our judicial system has operated for some years within the parameters of such strict legislation, with the result that we have developed a certain sophistication in handling problems of this nature. In order to provide for such judicial discretion, the limitation on pain and suffering is further expressly designated as not applicable whenever the injuries are such that the failure to award such damages would be considered unfair by the jury.

True, any such "loophole" may be subject to abuse. In this regard it is no different from the great body of the law in our society, which depends on proper and reasonable interpretation by the court, by the lawyers, and by the officers of the court, in its application. In view of the clear purpose of the limitation on pain and suffering under the Multiple Benefits Plan, the specific exemptions, and the expertise of our judicial system in determining matters of this nature, there is no reason to believe that this specific legislation would fail to function satisfactorily.

This limitation on pain and suffering, therefore, is intended to eliminate to a great degree the nuisance value of small tort claims. On the other hand, it is intended that full pain and suffering (or "general damages") awards would be available to victims in cases of actual injury.

Advance Payments

Many liability carriers have failed to make prompt advance payments to potential claimants because of a fear that such advance payments would appear later in a tort suit against their insured as evidence of admitted liability. The Multiple Benefits Plan expressly incorporates legislation providing that such advance payments would not constitute a waiver or an estoppel against the insurance carrier, and would be inadmissible in a later tort suit as evidence of liability. The result of this limitation should be to encourage such advance payments by liability carriers. Doubtless, this particular fear on the part of liability carriers is not the only reason that such payments have not been made in the past; but, accordingly, this change in the tort law is not the only change contained in the Multiple Benefits Plan in order to induce such payments by the companies.

Collateral Source Rule

Under the Collateral Source Rule, victims suing in tort are able to pray for damages for which they have already been compensated as a result of collateral sources. The Collateral Source Rule has two opposite consequences. First, in small claims, the nuisance value of the case might lead to a full, or even excessive, settlement by the liability insurer, despite the fact that the victim had already received compensation from other insurance or other sources. To the extent to which this diverts money from more needy victims in order to provide double recovery in these nuisance claims, it is clearly a part of the malapportionment of benefit problems. Second, individuals with large, catastrophic claims are enabled by the Collateral Source Rule to pray for full compensation from the negligent defendant even though they may have received other compensation from collateral sources. These individuals, however, are nevertheless very seldom fully compensated.

The Collateral Source Rule is not completely altered by the application of the Multiple Benefits Plan. The Rule would be altered by the application of the Multiple Benefits Plan. The Rule would be altered only insofar as it applies to tort suits by those victims who have first-party benefits payable to them under a Dual Protection automobile insurance policy. In such tort cases, these individuals will not be granted recovery representing compensation for injuries for which they have already been compensated as a result of their first-party insurance coverages under the Dual Protection Policy. This not only prevents double recovery, one from the Multiple Benefits Plan and the other from the tort suit, but also tends to lessen the degree of litigation, in that the tort claim filed by the individual victim in such cases would be reduced by the amount of benefits he has received. This reduction in the value of the tort claim would be of interest, of course, not only to the individual victim, but to any potential attorney considering his case on a contingent fee basis.

In other matters, the Collateral Source Rule remains unchanged. That is, individuals may still sue in tort for losses which have been compensated from collateral sources other than the Dual Protection Policy insurance. In practice the probability of double recovery in the smaller cases is greatly lessened by designating the Dual Protection Policy's first-party insurance as primary coverage. This designation would serve to prevent dual recoveries under the Personal Accident Benefit and outside first-party insurance coverages, because those other coverages would probably be designated as excess over the Dual Protection Policy's Personal Accident Benefit. This alteration would allow a reduction in premium; and so whenever lower premiums (and the accompanying increase in market penetration) were desired, this change would occur. At the same time, such insurance would still be available to a victim who is seriously injured, as excess insurance over the Personal Accident Benefit coverages, and would further result in the reduced premium for the extra benefit, with the first $2,000 of loss from automobile accidents paid under the Dual Protection Policy.

For those individuals with a catastrophic loss the system operates so that they might be compensated as fully as possible. Such individuals would be compensated first under their Personal Accident Benefit, to the maximum limits of their coverage, and second, by any additional insurance benefits which they had at their disposal. Because such individuals are very seldom fully compensated, the possibilities of their full recovery in tort would not necessarily, or probably, lead to an abuse of the system. (Note: This change in the Collateral Source Rule is unnecessary in this particular context; the subrogation principle would automatically insure against double recovery, because the victim would have transferred his right to those particular elements of recovery to the insurance company as a consequence of accepting the direct insurance benefits.)

Judicial Reform

The congested situation in some of our courts has been discussed. Throughout the majority of the jurisdictions there is no such delay and all cases are heard within a reasonable time after filing. In those jurisdictions where there is delay, it has frequently been overlooked that the delay is not the result of tort litigation, and even more especially not of automobile insurance litigation. In those jurisdictions where the court dockets are heavy, the congestion is the result of an unusually high backlog of criminal cases. Because of constitutional guarantees to citizens of the U.S., those citizens accused under the criminal law have a constitutional right to a "speedy" trial. Therefore civil suits, including automobile accident cases, are frequently put off again and again as new criminal cases are slipped into the docket as a matter of necessity.

The above situation is an indication that the solution to court delay in these jurisdictions does not lie in the field of automobile insurance reform. Automobile insurance claimants suffer from the delay; they do not create it. The answer to the delay must lie in the area of judicial reform. In many cases such reform may be relatively easy to accomplish. The keystone of the system may be an individual assignment system rather than a central assignment system. The central assignment system may reduce docket progress to the level of the slowest judges; and such a slowdown in the proceeding may be disastrous. Seminars may be used in order to apprise the judges of the tools at their disposal which may be used to eliminate the slowdown which is inherent in many modern legal cases. Primary among the tools given the judges may be the idea that reduction of delay is the personal responsibility of the judge from the moment the case is filed, and that it is the judge's duty to bring the case to conclusion within the least amount of time reasonable needed for that particular case. In order that the judges may proceed along this course rationally, it may be provided that the clerk should give semimonthly reports to each judge as to the status of each pending case. Finally, the responsibility should be placed upon the judge to control the case when in court. The judge must require proper pleadings and proper use of the continuance privilege. He must provide prompt and proper disposition of post-verdict or post-judgment motions as well as pre-verdict motions, and actively use the power to dismiss cases without prejudice for want of prosecution in appropriate instances, and require the use of trial briefs.

Delay in getting automobile accident cases to court has proved to be a problem in certain jurisdictions. While a problem in several large metropolitan areas, it is not a problem in many jurisdictions. Because of this disparity, judicial efficiency is a need in the operation of the present system which requires a solution which is flexible, allowing a cure to be applied where needed, and omitted where not needed. A method of resolving this difficulty which has met with some success is a system of compulsory arbitration of small claims.

Under such a system each claim may be subject to hearing by a panel of three arbitrators who, as members of the bar in the jurisdiction, have consented to serve as arbiters. The individual arbitrators are appointed by a court clerk and they hold their hearings at the convenience of the parties. Their decision has the effect of a final judgment, except that either party may appeal as a matter of right, upon repaying the county the cost of the arbitration proceedings. The costs are limited to an amount not in excess of 50% of the amount in controversy, and are usually in the $75-$100 range.

Such a plan in Pennsylvania has been in satisfactory operation for several years. Attacks upon its constitutionality have been unsuccessful. The success of the system is due in large part to the cooperation of the Bar in supplying skilled arbitrators at low cost. Arbitration, however, even though it has been found helpful in solving the delay problem in some areas, would in fact perhaps create a _burden_ in other areas where no delay problem exists. Arbitration, therefore, as included in the Multiple Benefits

Plan, should be available to be implemented in each individual state jurisdiction or subjurisdiction as needed, upon the recommendation of the state Attorney General or Insurance Commissioner, for use only in those areas of the state where such a need is seen, and this flexibility is an integral part of the Judicial Reform Proposal of the plan. Arbitration need not be instituted on a wholesale level, but should rather be instituted in order to solve specific problems where those problems arise.

The method of choosing arbitrators in the Philadelphia system has proven to be satisfactory. The costs have not been excessive, and the quality of justice does not appear to have suffered. To the extent that arbitration is used as a "spot" process, therefore, this method of choosing arbitrators should be preferred. At the same time, in those areas where delay is anticipated to be a permanent problem (or at least a semi-permanent problem), perhaps a more permanent solution should be implemented. It is suggested that Automobile Accident Arbitration Boards rather than arbitration panels individually created by each case, could be standing bodies designed for the hearing of automobile cases on a continuing basis. Thus a court of lower jurisdiction, similar to the "Family Courts," "Traffic Courts," or "Small Claims Courts," could be created to hear automobile cases. Instead of a paid judge to handle such a court, for instance, a panel of three arbitrators could be appointed by the governor, one from a list submitted by the trial Bar, one from a list submitted by the other two arbitrators. Such a board could be compensated on a fee basis, based upon cases heard, just as the individual arbitration courts in the Philadelphia plan, and such a system would doubtless lead to great efficiency in the disposition of small automobile claims. Any case could be appealed from this court of first jurisdiction merely upon payment of the appropriate appeal fee.

Competitive Rating

Insurance rates applicable under the Multiple Benefits Plan are determined by competition, in the open market, amongst the members of the insurance industry, under the Open Competition Rating Plan. Such competition has proven to be the most effective method of assuring fair pricing in the American marketplace. Rate competition has been spirited in that industry in recent years. Competition also serves to greatly lessen the possibility of an inadequate rate structure leading to insolvencies among the smaller companies, because such companies will be enabled to achieve the necessary market penetration required for their operations by serving the segments of the market which are not able to meet the strict underwriting requirements of the leaders in the price compeittion. In any event, the purpose of the system is assurance that the insurance companies will be able to respond to change in income potential and the market, so that they might implement rates unilaterally in an open system of free competition, with the rates to be filed for informational purposes with the Insurance Commission only as required at the time of company audit.

It is anticipated that the actual policy forms will differ very little from company to company. Just as the Family Automobile Policy is the standard automobile insurance form in the industry today, with minor variations amongst the various companies' versions thereof, so the general provisions of the Dual Protection Policy would be standard, including both the liability coverages and the Personal Accident Benefit. The degree of policy differences from company to company would likely remain much the same as at present.

However, even so, the actual segment of the market available to each of the different companies might vary tremendously. Under a system of open competition, those companies so desiring would be able to practice a policy of strict underwriting, in such a way that their underwriting losses could be minimized, so that they would be able to bring their policies to the market at the lowest possible premium. Such companies would have to consider only their own expenses, their own collateral income, and their own underwriting results, in determining their rates, rather than being influenced by the conduct of other, possibly less efficient, insurance companies. Hopefully this might result in some lowering of insurance rates.

Even to the extent, however, that the lowest rates available to the public were not greatly changed, a competition rating system would be desirable because it would enable a larger percentage of the insurance industry to bring its policies to the vast number of "lower risk" segments of the market at low premiums.

The results should be, at the very least, that a larger percentage of the public will be able to obtain low-cost insurance. At the same time, the high-risk segment of the market would similarly be served by such an open competition rating system. Individuals in this category would find insurance protection available to them in the voluntary insurance market; their desired coverage would be available at a cost approximating its true cost.

Obviously the very highest-risk drivers will, as a rule, be always unable to "carry their own load" in regard to premiums, because such premiums would price the insurance completely beyond their abilities to pay. To this very limited extent, therefore, high-risk drivers would receive the benefit of somewhat less realistic rates than some other members of the remainder of the insurance pool. At the same time, however, a system of open competition would allow for greater <u>flexibility</u> in rates, so that the individuals in this favored classification would only be those individuals who truly presented so great a risk. Open competition serves the dual purpose of reducing the need for the premiums of low-risk drivers to reflect the loss experience of higher-risk drivers, and lowering the premiums charges those drivers who are now forced to obtain insurance through Assigned Risk Plans, because these individuals, presenting a risk somewhat higher than normal but yet within the bounds of financial feasibility, would purchase their insurance at a premium approximating its true cost. The result of the system, in its entirety, therefore, should be that a very large segment of the insurance buying public is able to obtain insurance through the voluntary insurance market, at lower premiums.

A collateral benefit, of yet very great importance, is that open rate competition serves to spur greater efficiency in the insurance industry itself. In the first place, insurance companies would be economically unable, for rate-making purposes, to separate underwriting profit from investment profit, inasmuch as each company would have to seize upon <u>any</u> source of income in its rate determinations in order to establish a premium which, in conjunction with its underwriting philosophy, would enable it to receive a substantially large portion of the available business.

A further result of the same considerations, therefore, is that insurance companies would be induced to operate with greater efficiency. Just as all income could be used to lower rates - therefore ultimately leading to a greater market penetration by the company - so could greater efficiency within the insurance organization itself lead to these same results. To the extent to which an insurance company is able to operate efficiently, with low overhead and low incidental expenses, such operations would result in savings which could be reflected in the rates charged by that insurance company to its policyholders. A highly efficient organization would be able to charge the lowest rates. Other companies, to the extent to which this degree of efficiency was impossible, would be forced to charge higher premiums for their policies, thereby achieving their market penetration among other drivers by the adoption of realistic underwriting standards. This operation of the system should prove a powerful spur for the insurance industry to increase its own efficiency. At the same time, it would enable certain companies which can serve a worthwhile function in providing full market availability, including substandard insurers, to continue to operate in that market, inasmuch as substandard risks would be able to be insured under the voluntary market under an appropriate premium rate.

Solvency Assurance

Insolvencies amongst insurance companies are not only rare, but are virtually unknown among the more substantial companies. The result, therefore, is that a very small segment of the insurance market is very directly affected by the threat of company insolvency. Even so, some concern has been generated by the possibility of policyholder loss resulting from insolvencies. Any company which might become insolvent would likely be very small, and would therefore likely penetrate a very small segment of the insurance market. Concern has been generated, however, and a system must be established so that no member of the insurance-buying public will suffer from the insolvency of an insurance company, either through loss of premiums or through loss of coverage upon presentation of a claim.

The Multiple Benefits Plan includes legislation creating a plan guaranteeing that no member of the consumer public will suffer, in either way, from the insolvency of an insurance company. This legislation operates to create the "Automobile Insurance Industry Solvency Assurance Plan," with the members of the plan being all companies (domestic and foreign) doing business within the jurisdiction. Such a plan, therefore, will have the entire economic power and weight of the state's insurance industry behind it. The plan is administered by the insurance industry itself, through a governing board, in accordance with appropriate regulation by the state Insurance Commission.

In operation, the plan requires that, when insolvency of any company doing business in the state is determined, all members of the plan should be assessed an appropriate amount in order to meet the obligations of the insolvent company, in order to acquire the necessary funds, on pro-rata basis, amongst the members of the plan. Inasmuch as all insurance companies doing business in the state would be required to be members of the compact, this assessment on the basis of premiums written in the state would rationally apportion this cost amongst the members of the industry. In order to prevent a disproportionate hardship upon very small companies, the maximum assessment to any company under the plan in any one calendar year should be limited to one percent of premiums written. To the extent to which any very small company would by this limitation avoid fulfilling all its obligation, that obligation would be spread amongst the other members of the industry. Thus, without creation of any "fund," with its bureaucratic organization and machinery, the public's need will have been met.

The operation of the Plan would enable the insurance industry to meet the "solvency assurance need" in a sure, certain, stable, and reliable manner. Accommodation of this need under the Multiple Benefits Plan will make certain that all members of the industry participate, with individual company responsibility proprotionate to the business written in the state. Further, the financial strength of the entire industry will meet the obligations of any single company difficulties. At the same time, this need is filled without the creation of a new and unnecessary bureaucracy, and without adding to the expense of the system through the inefficiencies and internal expenses which such a bureaucracy would create. Because the assessment upon the insurance companies occurs when the funds are needed, rather than in advance, the insurance industry will retain these funds as it operates, with the income from the investment of the funds going to the compa-

nies, to be considered in reducing the premium rates to be paid
by the insurance buying public. Thus the entire financial operation of the industry will be further devoted to serve the public
good. The result should be a combination of assured solvency
and the lowering of premium rates, in accordance with the other
principles of the Multiple Benefits Plan.

Meeting the financial needs of the public and industry in the
event of an insolvency would solve only half the problem, however.
The other facet of the problem is the prevention of financial responsibility in the insurance industry. In this regard, the "Automobile Insurance Industry Solvency Assurance Plan" required
each insurer member of the plan to be periodically audited by an
independent certified public accounting agency, in order that the
financial solvency of the company might be ascertained. Such
audits will be reported to the governing board of the plan, and
the governing board will not only be allowed, but required, to
report to the State Insurance Department concerning the financial condition and situation of the members of the compact. In
the event of the sound financial operation, such report need only
be affirmative, but in the event that a company's financial soundness is questionable, the full report should be available to the Insurance Department in order for regulation to be appropriately
administered.

The operation of such a plan should not only serve to greatly reduce the effects on any insolvencies amongst the members
of the insurance industry, so that the present minimal level of
insolvencies could be reduced to almost nothing (and to absolutely
nothing in the jurisdiction in the area of the policyholder loss)
but such a plan could operate to lower further the cost of uninsured motorist protection. Uninsured motorist protection, of
course, has been held to be applicable in the event that the tort-
feasor is liable, and was insured at the time of the accident, but
the insurance is not payable because of the insolvency of his insurance carrier. Insolvency of the insurance carrier, under the
"Automobile Insurance Industry Solvency Assurance Plan," would
be of effect only outside the jurisdiction where the Multiple Benefits Plan was enacted, inasmuch as the obligations of a techni-
cally "insolvent" carrier would be assumed by the governing
board of the plan so that the "insolvency" would not exist as a
matter of fact at all within the jurisdiction. Under such circum-

stances, the uninsured motorist protection would not be relied
upon to pay such claims, because they would be payable in full
by the industry, through the plan. This reduction in potential
loss under the uninsured motorist coverage should serve to reduce
those premiums, already extremely reasonable, to new lows.

Of course, to the extent to which drivers with Dual Protection Policies were active in jurisdictions where the Multiple Benefits Plan was not in effect, they would still be able to rely upon their uninsured motorist protection in the event that their claim was unenforceable only against an insolvent insurance company. In essence, uninsured motorists protection would be made extra-territorial for those motorists within the jurisdiction of the Multiple Benefits Plan, because the insolvency problem would no longer exist; and neither would the problem of other uncollectible tort judgments, as explained in conjunction with the "Assigned Liability Claims Plan," if feasible.

Chapter Nine

ADDITIONAL LEGISLATION INCLUDED
(CONTINUED)

Market Availability

One of the great difficulties in the operation of the present system results from the inability of all licensed drivers to obtain the necessary insurance coverages. The problem is the result of three different factors. First, certain individuals are unable to obtain coverage because they represent such a substandard risk that no insurance company is willing to write their business. It is unquestionably a social value which must be served that all individuals who are allowed to drive under our present licensing and registration system should have access to appropriate insurance coverages, both sufficient first-party insurance coverages and appropriate ancilliary coverages.

An initial and primary step in the solution of this difficulty must be the more socially rational implementation of the driver licensing process. The real need is that of removing dangerous drivers as a threat on the highway. Thus the Multiple Benefits Plan includes legislation implementing the beginning of an organized and comprehensive effort to develop a realistic appraisal of the characteristics by which the danger can be curbed, and techniques whereby their contribution to the risk of automobile accidents may be lessened without interference with their basic right to freedom and mobility.

In order to alleviate this condition (that is, that some individuals because they present a substandard risk are unable to obtain liability coverages), Assigned Risk Plans have been instituted. Under such plans, these individuals, when they determine that they are unable to obtain insurance on the voluntary market, proceed through the Plan and are assigned to an insurance company participating in the Plan. That company will then write liability insurance for them. The theory, of course, is that even to the extent that these individuals represent a high risk, they should be allowed to obtain insurance as long as they are allowed to drive. By assigning the risk proportionately among the various companies participating in the system, it is hoped that the accompanying high risk, and the necessary deviation from the principle of risk-related rates, will be spread evenly among the insurance buying public through the insurance company mechanism. Unfortunately, the Assigned Risk Plans have not functioned adequately in meeting the problem because of the supposed "stigma" attached to obtaining insurance through the assigned risk program. Inasmuch as some substandard drivers are substandard not because of their prior accident driving record, but because of other factors which are reasonable but not publicly recognized as morally reprehensible, this process has created some resentment.

Secondly, even to the extent that these individuals are able to obtain insurance through the assigned risks program, the companies to which they are assigned have only been required to provide them with the basic coverages which may be demanded under the state's financial responsibility law. As a result, these individuals have usually only been able to purchase the very lowest limits of liability insurance coverage, and they have similarly not usually had access to the first-party or other optional coverages.

Thirdly, even to the extent that these individuals are allowed to buy insurance, as it is limited, through the assigned risk system, such insurance is likely to prove very expensive. However, in accordance with a rational and morally appropriate allocation of costs, it is to be expected that these individuals should be charged higher premiums for their insurance than low-risk drivers. But the entire purpose of the insurance system is defeated to the extent that the premiums charged these individuals are so high and unreasonable that the individuals in the end are unable to obtain the insurance.

In order to solve this market availability problem as it exists in the present system, certain goals should be kept in mind. The present system has served quite well in certain of its aspects. For example, each individual insured is assigned to a company who classifies and rates him so as to achieve for him the maximum reasonable premiums. Upon presentation of a claim, it behooves that company to investigate closely the claim so that claim expenses and payments are only those which are necessary and proper. Both of these activities on the part of the company to which an assigned risk motorist is assigned tend to increase the efficiency of the system, and decrease the degree to which those high-risk drivers impose higher costs upon the remainder of the motoring public. Also, to the degree to which the assigned risks program provides that all companies shall participate, the cost of the high-risk driver in handling his applications in claims, is spread on a proportionate basis throughout the industry, on the basis of premiums written. Through the same mechanism, the extra cost of subsidizing such drivers is spread equitably among the insurance-buying public.

A third advantage of the present system is that the loss ratios incurred by these high risk drivers are realistically reflected in the individual company's rates. This allows the experience of the substandard drivers to be calculated integrally in the rate computations of the various companies. Where rates are controlled by a state insurance commission, this experience is valuable in determining an appropriate rate level. Under the open competition rating system of the Multiple Benefits Plan, companies would have to use their experience with their substandard drivers in their calculations in determination of their rates. Furthermore, particularly in regard to the open rate competition under the Multiple Benefits Plan, it is intended that the various companies with their styles of underwriting, therefore greatly increasing the proportion of automobile business which is absorbed in the voluntary market.

Under the "Expanded Automobile Insurance Availability Plan" of the Multiple Benefits Plan, individuals who are informed that they are unable to obtain insurance under the voluntary insurance market, will also be informed that they will be able to obtain insurance through the availability plan. Such individuals need only meet the requirements of the plan, which are (1) an application in good faith, (2) a valid driver's license, and (3) payment of the premium obligation.

Individuals would be able to obtain, through the Expanded Automobile Insurance Availability Plan, liability up to the $50,000-$100,000-$10,000 level. (Such maximum limit levels are much more in line with the needs of these individuals than the artificially low levels established by most state financial responsibility laws, even though those artificially low levels should be increased under the Multiple Benefits Plan financial responsibility plan.)

They would also be able to receive collision and comprehensive insurance, with deductibles, of no less than $100, with appropriate vehicle age and maximum value limitations. These individuals would naturally receive the automatic first-party benefits of the Multiple loss benefits, and the survivor's benefits, with these benefits being identical to those provided by the voluntary insurance market.

An additional advantage of this plan is that all segments of the industry will be participating. To the extent to which companies write only collision and comprehensive coverages, these companies would be able to participate in the plan, because certain individuals would be wanting to obtain these specific coverages. This, again, would provide for a better allocation of cost among the companies and among the insurance-buying public.

An additional advantage of the Expanded Automobile Insurance Availability Plan is that, once again in conjunction with the open competition rating, it tends to point up the real cost of allowing unqualified drivers to operate motor vehicles. To the extent to which this cost is considered unduly burdensome, perhaps legislatures will be motivated to provide more realistic methods of testing and licensing drivers.

Omnibus Protection

The Dual Protection Policy contains the traditional "Omnibus Clause" normally found in the Family Automobile Policy today. In addition, however, the Dual Protection Policy's omnibus clause will extend the first-party coverages of the policy to pedestrians who are injured as the result of an accident in which the insured vehicle is involved, regardless of fault, if the pedestrian is a member of a non-car-owning household and has therefore not had the Dual Protection Policy made available to him.

Assigned Liability Claims

In order to obtain the benefits of the operation of the tort law system and achieve a morally appropriate allocation of costs and a deterrence of negligent driving, it is necessary that valid tort law "negligence" judgments be collectible. Such judgments are collectible from and against the individual, of course, and if he is judgment-proof, against his liability carrier. In the event that a judgment-proof individual does not carry liability insurance, an individual may proceed under the provisions of the uninsured motorist coverage in his own Family Automobile Policy or Dual Protection Policy. The individual who declines to purchase such coverage may be able to obtain a valid tort judgment which is uncollectible, and so some provision must be made in order to make these judgments collectible, while allocating the costs appropriately.

In order to meet this need, such claims under the Multiple Benefits Plan will be assigned (proportionately to premiums written by the automobile industry in the jurisdiction, or at least among that segment of the industry writing liability insurance) just as the present "assigned risks" drivers are. It will be up to the individual companies faced with the claim to determine the disposition of the claims in accordance with normal claims practice, as though it had insured the driver, subject of course to a maximum liability equal to the financial responsibility laws of the jurisdiction. The company will settle the claim with the victim, defending against the claim if it feels the claim is invalid.

The plaintiff, in such a case, will bring suit against the defendant driver. The company to which the claim is assigned will, of course, have no obligation to defend the driver, but may do so if it wishes. To the extent to which the victim has the Dual Protection Policy's Personal Accident Benefit available to him, the liability carrier to which the case is assigned will be spurred to settle the claim reasonably. Under such an "Assigned Liability Claims Plan" it is imperative that the company to which the claim is assigned have full rights of subrogation against the negligent third party, and that the company pursue their subrogation rights. This subrogation operation will prevent motorists from feeling that they can decline to purchase liability insurance coverage on the basis that such coverage will be forthcoming if they are involved in an accident.

Insurance companies maintain staffs of attorneys for other purposes, and it will be no great burden on these companies for them to pursue their subrogation claims diligently and continually. Such pursuit should be required legislatively unless viewed as not necessary.

In many states where liability insurance is not required (and where, of course, an Assigned Liability Claims Plan is not in operation), upwards of 95-96% of all motorists carry liability coverage. This percentage has not been increased significantly in those states where insurance has been made compulsory, and there will always be those few individuals who manage to circumvent the system. The Assigned Liability Claims Plan accomplishes the same objective as Compulsory Insurance, in that individuals who are not of a basic criminal nature will be strongly urged to purchase liability coverage. Yet, under this plan those individuals who absolutely refuse to do so will retain that freedom of choice and action, without being able to pass the result, or the ultimate costs, of their personal actions on to the victims of their negligence if they are responsible for injuries.

Public Information and Education

There is a good deal of educated opinion to the effect that the public does not fully understand the basis of the present system. Public opinion polls have indicated that the public agrees that fault, or negligence, should play a part in the determination of who should pay for automobile accidents, or who should bear a greater proportion of the costs through the cost allocation mechanism of the insurance industry. It is imperative, therefore, that the public be apprised of the fact that the present system, and particularly the Multiple Benefits Plan, with its improvements, tends to further these very values. This need is met by the Public Information and Education Model incorporated in the plan.

Accident Prevention Program

Accident prevention is the concern of all segments of society. One of the goals of the Multiple Benefits Plan is to place the insurance industry in a position of leadership in achieving a better accident prevention record. Therefore the plan includes the Automobile Accident Prevention Model, a program of research designed to pinpoint the causes of accidents, with appropriate follow-up authority for the implementation of additional legislation directed at accident prevention, based upon the results of the research. The National Highway Safety Act, is a preliminary step in the direction which must be followed, but there is no evidence that the particular reforms included in that legislation are actually effective in accident prevention. Future legislation should be much more carefully conceived and drafted, with sufficient supportive empirical research.

Some states have instituted motor vehicle inspection laws, in an attempt to insure that all vehicles driven on the highways meet certain standards in regard to certain of the vehicles' characteristics. Generally, these vehicle inspection laws require inspection and correction, if necessary, of headlight alignment, brake linings, vision through the windshield, and other similar tests, and there is slight evidence that these programs have contributed to lowering the accident loss rate when implemented. Such evidence as exists is statistical and does not show any clear cause and effect relationship, furthermore, and the program continues to be controversial.

It is important that the pros and cons of such programs be analyzed carefully. Undoubtedly there is merit in any inspection system which, at a socially acceptable price, apprises motor vehicle owners of any serious deficiencies in the mechanical condition of their automobiles. At the same time, it cannot be denied that there are abundant opportunities for abuse in such systems where the defects, when located, must be immediately repaired. Probably it is this probability of abuse which leads to public opposition to the programs.

The Multiple Benefits Plan encourages empirical research into this and other safety areas, in order to determine how best to lower the accident rate. It may be that mere inspection, without repairs, thereby apprising motor vehicle owners of the deficiencies in their automobile, will suffice to lower the accident rate.

Generally speaking, negligence, in automobile accident cases, has been no more difficult to prove in court than have other legal issues. There is no evidence to support the contention that automobile accidents occur as a result of anything other, as a general rule, than controllable human behavior (including that of the highway designer, automobile maker, and others, as well as the driver). Therefore, the Multiple Benefits Plan adheres to the traditional values of deterrence and rational allocation of costs in an attempt to complement the criminal law in deterring negligent behavior on the part of drivers, as well as to encourage safe highway design and design of automobiles that are safer to drive and safer to ride in. Only by allocating the cost in accordance with these factors, bringing economic pressure on the driver, will the true cost of motoring be brought to the attention of the public so that the corrective measures will in fact be implemented.

Evolutionary Progress

No radical changes should be made while the public does not understand the present system. It is unrealistic to determine that the public is dissatisfied with the present system and wants a change, when research and scholarly opinion indicates that the public is dissatisfied not with the present system, but with their uneducated opinion of how the present system works. The extent of change which may be required, or the direction which it should take, cannot be properly ascertained on the basis of public opinion until such time as the public understands the operations of the present system and the goals to be sought.

Consistent with the recognition of the fact that the public feels that fault should play a definite part in the determination of who should bear the cost for automobile accidents, the Multiple Benefits Plan continues the beneficial operation of the tort system. Thus allocation of costs are morally appropriate to the degree that high-risk drivers bear a proportionately greater cost of the accident problem than do low-risk drivers. However, at the same time, it is clear that the public, in the 1970's, feels that all victims of automobile accidents should be compensated to some degree. The Multiple Benefits Plan provides the benefit that all victims can recover, but at the same time maintains a differential between the amount of recovery provided for victims who are at fault for their own injuries and individuals who are not.